THE CHRISTIAN OUTLOOK

THE CHRISTIAN
OUTLOOK

By

KENNETH SCOTT LATOURETTE

D. Willis James Professor of Missions and
Oriental History and Fellow of
Berkeley College in Yale University

NEW YORK *and* LONDON

HARPER & BROTHERS PUBLISHERS

CONTENTS

PREFACE

THIS book is an attempt to think through the most pressing
problem of a crucial era. To those who live in them most
ages seem central and critical. This conviction has been right.
Again and again the human race has been in peril and has
seemed on the verge of disaster. Again and again, too, it has
appeared to the contemporaries to be on the eve of a great new
day. Always it has survived, even though with tragic losses and
as "by the skin of its teeth." Never, moreover, have the roseate
hopes of the dreamers been completely fulfilled. Neither the
prophets of doom nor the confident dreamers of the heavenly
city have been entirely justified by the event. Yet each great age
has been critical. Upon its outcome has depended in large part
the course of the succeeding ages. Those who viewed it as deter-
minative were not entirely wrong.

Our age is peculiarly crucial. It is no absorption with our
own concerns, our own egocentrism, and our unsupportable
conviction that the ages have been culminated in us, which lead
us to say so. Nor is it a lack of historical perspective which is
responsible. Indeed, historical perspective impels us to that conclusion. Never before has mankind been so closely knit by physical ties. Our shrunken world, made by the airplane and the
radio so much smaller than even that of the dawn of the century,
has brought the human race together more intimately in the
bundle of life than at any earlier time. This means that disorders
in any part affect the whole. The race rises or falls together. In
earlier ages disasters have overwhelmed one segment of man-

kind which have left other segments untouched. Advances have
reached only small portions of the globe. In our day humanity
falls or rises together. Mankind can be hurtled down into a state
worse than primitive barbarism or it can achieve greater richness of life for the whole.

In this decisive age the central issue is the course of the Christian faith. In the Gospel the ideal goal of man is set forth—to
be perfect as God is perfect, to be filled unto all the fullness of
God. It is thus that man attains the high destiny to which God
has called him. Failure to do so is to fall short of what God
means life to be. The future of Christianity is the future of
mankind.

Is the Gospel to be an increasing or a waning factor in the
collective life of man? Is it to be a dwindling current in the continuing stream of history? Is it to grow in power but still contend with other, conflicting currents? Is it fully to triumph? Can
we look for progress, even though by slow and uneven stages, to
the complete realization of the kingdom of God, as so many in
the nineteenth century hoped? Does evil become more rampant
until God intervenes to destroy the present order and by His
own fiat in judgment separate the bad from the good and, from
the latter, inaugurate His kingdom? Or do wheat and tares persist, with neither triumphing over the other and both following
out their logical growth until some sure but distant harvest?

What forms is the Gospel to take? In what institutional and
visible garbs will it be incarnated? Will the churches go on as
we have known them? If not, what modifications or innovations
will we see? Will growth be especially marked in one of the historic expressions of Christianity? If so, which?

It is questions such as these which are of prime importance
for the human race. It is with them that this book is concerned.

The approach is historical. It is from the perspective of the past that we attempt to look into the future. From the viewpoint of the long distances we endeavor to understand the changing present scene and to ascertain the direction in which currents are setting.

Moreover, it is from the basis of Christian conviction that these pages are written. Any account of the human scene must be from a particular viewpoint. All portrayals must be interpretations. Some elements are inevitably stressed and others minimized. Those who, in the name of scientific objectivity, profess to produce an account of the human race, either its history or its current manifestations, which is without bias are either self-deceived or dishonest. The following chapters are founded upon a profound belief in the self-revelation of God in Christ; that in Christ God sets forth the true goal of man, the goal which He has designed man to attain; that man, through a corruption which has distorted him, is of himself unable to attain that goal; that in Christ God has worked and works for the redemption of man, to enable man to do what, because of his sin, man cannot do of himself, namely, move toward the "goal of the high calling of God in Christ Jesus"; that here and now men, through faith, can enter upon the new life made possible by God's self-giving love, and, through God's love, be born into eternal life of growing fellowship and likeness with God; that here men can enter the kingdom of God and become members of that society whose ideal it is perfectly to do the will of God.

We are not attempting the intellectual validation of the Christian conviction. So far as that can be done it has often been accomplished. Experience has proved that no one reaches that conviction purely by the way of reason. Reason can assist, but conviction finally comes through a complete self-giving in trust. That faith is here assumed, for, presumably, the large majority who read these pages already are committed to it.

Yet that faith must not be an excuse for shutting our eyes to palpable facts, even when, to the Christian, they are unpleasant. We must try to see history as it actually has been and the current scene as it really is. On the basis of a frank and fearless facing of the world, frank and fearless because of confidence in Him who is the truth, we are to endeavor to look into the future.

Prophecy is notoriously fallible. "As for prophecy, it will pass away," we are told. That is the more sobering because of the added warning, "As for knowledge, it will pass away." Our view of the facts on which we seek to base our prophecy is also subject to error. Moreover, the past does not fully determine the future. It conditions and modifies it, but not beyond alterations, some of them profound. God has given to man a measure, even though a limited measure, of free will. Man in part can shape his own future.

We must act. To act we must seek to understand current trends. Current trends emerge from the trends of yesterday and the day before. We cannot unfailingly plot the direction which movements will take, but we know that they will follow out of antecedent movements. As we seek to understand the events of our day we can discern the fashion in which they followed earlier movements. Because of the many factors involved and the numbers of ways in which these can combine to produce tomorrow, we cannot always be sure of the details or even of all the main features of tomorrow. Besides, by our actions here and now we can modify tomorrow. But not all prophecy is futile. Much of it has high value and is in part validated by the outcome. Take, for example, the forecast made near the beginning of the present century that the two great powers of the latter part of the century were to be Russia and the United States. That has been amply fulfilled. But in 1900 no one, not even the wisest and most prescient, would have foreseen the kind of government under which Russia has so strikingly achieved that prominence.

While, then, we must be modest in our forecasts, we must not dodge the demand that we essay them. Especially should we look to the historian for guidance. Presumably, because of his familiarity with the past, his acquaintance with the ways in which earlier events have followed upon a still more remote past, and his knowledge of the errors and confirmations of prophecies, he should be in a position to guide his fellows as they attempt to look ahead.

The following chapters have been given in whole or in part as sets of lectures. In one form or another they were used for the Schneder Lectureship at the Theological Seminary of the Evangelical and Reformed Church at Lancaster, Pennsylvania, in September, 1946, as the Hyde Lectures at Andover-Newton Theological Seminary in October, 1946, as the Powell Lectures at the Canadian School of Missions in January, 1947, as the Holland Lectures at the Southwestern Baptist Theological Seminary in February, 1947, at the Eastern Baptist Theological Seminary in March, 1947, as the Moore Lectures at the San Francisco Theological Seminary at San Anselmo, California, in April, 1947, at Mercer University in June, 1947, as the Edward Cadbury Lectures at the University of Birmingham in the Michaelmas term of 1947 and at Cambridge University and at Regent's Park College, Oxford, in that same term. To all of these institutions the author is deeply indebted. He remembers with gratitude the courteous hearing and the stimulus of inquiring minds and of friendly criticisms and comments. To each and all of these institutions and to the founders of these lectureships he would express his profound gratitude.

Moreover, the author is under willing obligation to friends who have generously read parts or all of the manuscript and who have made comments which have been of assistance in the final revision, especially to Leland S. Albright, Robert S. Bilheimer, W. Richey Hogg, and John F. Merrill. Particularly would he acknowledge the aid of Mrs. Charles T. Lincoln who typed the manuscript and made suggestions as to literary style.

THE CHRISTIAN OUTLOOK

CHAPTER I

BY WAY OF INTRODUCTION: THE PROBLEM STATED

Is Christianity a passing phenomenon? Seen against the long background of history must we regard it as relatively transient? It is nearly two thousand years old, but viewed from the perspective of man's course on the planet, two millenniums are but a moment. Even when put against the measuring stick of the ten or fifteen thousand years which is the brief dimension of civilization thus far they are not long.

Or is Christianity a growing factor in the life of mankind? As a movement in history is it, so far as we can judge, only in its infancy?

If this latter is the correct viewpoint, and in the following chapters we shall be seeing reasons for believing that it is, what direction is Christianity probably to follow? Our knowledge is too limited to forecast with precision the far future. Even had we full information of the past and of our own times, we might not be able to foretell exactly the course which Christianity is to take. Back of these questions lies the agelong but ever pertinent issue of determinism as against indeterminism, of man's free will as against God's foreknowledge and God's decrees. In general, as we suggested in the preface, man has free will, very limited to be sure, but sufficient to modify his future, perhaps drastically. Since this is so, we cannot be completely certain of details or even of the main outcome within history. Yet we can tell what the course has thus far been and can plot the main trends and suggest where they seem to be leading.

How far can we, in our generation, help to shape the course which Christianity is to pursue? Can we do anything about it? If so, what?

These are issues which must concern every thoughtful Christian. They are especially of moment to those, whether clerical or lay, who are in any sense charged with the responsibility of leadership in the Church. They are also pertinent for the rank and file. All of us share in both the obligation and the privilege of representing Christ and of helping make possible the continuing witness to him, his life, and his power.

In this opening chapter we must seek to elaborate somewhat further the questions which we have propounded. They are the subject of this book. To them we will recur again and again. At the outset we must endeavor to understand them and to see what is involved in them.

I

Is Christianity a passing phenomenon? Is it a religion, a movement which has made a contribution to the race but which, for one reason or another, is being discarded? Is it a dwindling and transient phase of mankind's long pilgrimage?

Much in the historical scene appears to support an affirmative answer. It seems to be true of religions that they rise, expand, and wane. Some completely disappear. Others continue, but with slowly diminishing influence.

The thirteen centuries between 650 B.C. and A.D. 650 were especially marked by the emergence of the great religious systems which since then have spread until they have commanded the allegiance of the large majority of mankind. They included the Buddha, Confucius, the Christ, Mani, Mohammed, and possibly Zoroaster. They saw the flowering of the mystery cults, of Greek philosophy, and of the religious currents, such as Neo-

platonism, which issued from Greek thought or were influenced
by it. They witnessed the culmination of the line of great Hebrew prophets and the formulation of what we now think of as
Judaism. They spanned the development of Jainism, Taoism,
and Shinto. Hinduism antedated this period, but in its present
form it is largely the creation of these centuries. Such writings
as the Mahabharata, the Ramayana, and the Bhagavadgita date
from them. It was during these thirteen hundred years that the
Buddhism of India was largely reabsorbed into Hinduism, with
the attendant modification of the latter. Here, in this relatively
brief space of time, was a burst of creative religious activity. It
had its roots in earlier centuries. It continued in succeeding
centuries, but in these centuries it had its flowering.

After a period of creative thought and life and of geographic
spread, all these religions except Christianity became stagnant
and some of them disappeared. Buddhism still claims the allegiance of millions, but at least five centuries have elapsed since
it has made any marked territorial advance and fully that long
a time has passed since any major new current of creative life
and thought has issued from it. For more than a thousand years
Buddhism has been slowly declining in China, the largest of the
lands outside of India where it has been widely influential. In
India itself, the land of its birth and most prolific development,
it gradually yielded ground to Hinduism and eventually was
entirely displaced or absorbed by the latter. Such Buddhism as
is to be found today in India is a reimportation by immigration
or is in border communities. Confucianism has never spread far
outside the circle of Chinese cultural influence. It has produced
no outstanding figure since Chu Hsi, in the twelfth century,
nearly seven hundred and fifty years ago, and Chu Hsi was not
so much a creator as a synthesizer of earlier creative systems—
Taoism, Buddhism, and Confucianism. In the present century

Confucianism has been dealt body blows through the passing of the imperial structure and the related system of education which were based upon it and which were the chief means of its perpetuation. Manichaeism rose, spread widely across Europe, Northern Africa, and Asia, and completely disappeared. Islam still flourishes, but its great territorial advances were made within nine hundred years of its birth. A few new movements emerged from it in the nineteenth century, but for original, vigorous thought or depth of religious life and insight they have not begun to approach the achievements of earlier centuries. What we call Zoroastrianism never, as a formal cult, spread far outside the Persian stock. It persists only among the Parsees, small minorities in India and Persia. The mystery religions have long since vanished. So completely have they gone that we know them only imperfectly. Greek philosophy continues to exert a marked influence and still underlies much of Occidental thought. Yet, apart from Christianity, since the Neoplatonists it has thrown up no figure of the first water, and the Neoplatonists, by their very name, were secondary to Socrates and Plato. Judaism has continued and is still stalwart, but not for over a millennium has it produced a great religious genius and not for centuries has it been the major stimulus, apart from Christianity, to first-class philosophy. It has been a narrow stream, strictly confined within the Jewish community, resistant, but in these latter decades suffering severely from the corrosion of secularism. Millions of those who call themselves Jews have given up all but a few formal remnants of their historic faith. Never since the great prophets and codifiers of its laws gave it form has it suffered such wholesale apostasy. Jainism has gone on, but in a narrow groove and without striking new life. Taoism has produced no major figure for over fifteen hundred years and has survived partly through inertia, partly because of its borrowing from Buddhism, partly through its catering to a demand of near-primitive minds for exorcism of evil spirits, and partly because its early classics still make an appeal to a few thoughtful and spiritually hungry souls. Shinto enjoyed a revival in the nineteenth century, but this was because of its use by the Japanese state for political purposes and because, in crude popular cults, it entered a vacuum left by the slow decay of Buddhism and because of the appeal of these sects to a widely spread craving for magic. Not for many centuries has Hinduism registered notable geographic extension and where it once enjoyed a wide vogue, in Southeastern Asia and the East Indies, it has been all but eliminated. Within India itself it remains vigorous, but even there the acids of modernity are dissolving the religious convictions of some of its more highly educated adherents.

Sikhism presents an apparent exception to this general picture. It was born far after the period which we have suggested as that of the major faiths of mankind. Indeed, it appeared more than eight centuries after A.D. 650. It has recently grown rapidly in the numbers of its adherents. Yet it has in it nothing basically revolutionary in religion and it has been confined almost entirely to India.

Why was the birth of so many of the high religions primarily in these brief thirteen centuries? Why is it that their course has been marked by rise and decay? Is it because, like individuals, or, better still, cultures, they have their youth, maturity, old age, and eventual death? Or is it because religion itself is a stage through which mankind passes? Is the explanation to be found in the movement of mankind from what we usually call "primitive" religion to more "advanced" systems and then from them away from religion entirely? Is mankind now moving forward, as some pre-1914 optimistic humanists or their belated successors would assure us, into a bright age of scientific emancipation from religion, into a larger freedom which needs no religion, or, if the new age has religion, into religions far different from anything which has previously gone by that name? Or, as much of pre-Christian thoughtful mankind held, does history go by meaningless cycles and are we now on the downsweep of disintegration toward a negation of the values of high religion and toward barbarism? Or, as we Christians would like to believe, is the disappearance of the older faiths because these systems are being displaced by the final religion, Christianity? In which of these answers, if any, lies the explanation of this strange record?

We must say at once that none of the answers which we have put in the form of questions fully explains the fact. We must reply, in the main, that we do not know the full reasons.

The explanation is not to be found in a parallel to the life course of an individual. Religion and an individual man are so different that the similarity must be more superficial than real.

Nor is the doctrine of progress sound. We do not know what the religions of the earliest men were. We cannot prove that they were the same as those of modern "primitives" or even closely akin to them. Even if the religions of modern "primitives" are those of early man, the advance to the "high" religions is not necessarily followed by movement to a still more advanced stage. The modern paganisms which combine secularism, nationalism, and social theories seem to be regressions rather than advances. They certainly are regressions when measured against Christian standards.

The cyclical hypothesis of history is also unsatisfactory. Man makes advances in many realms, even though unevenly.

Moreover, the decay of religions is not always correlated with the advance of science. In some religions the decline had begun before the appearance of science and its associated secular mind.

The latter have simply hastened a decay which was already in process. The appearance of the machine and of the science which gave rise to it has been followed by the disintegration of "primitive" cultures and their associated religions. But the stagnation of Islam and Confucianism and the slow decline of Buddhism had begun long before modern science was born. The coming of the latter has at most hastened what had already commenced.

The spread of Christianity is not the full answer. Christianity has displaced some polytheisms and animistic cults, but, except in the Graeco-Roman world, it has seldom made marked gains from other "high" religions. It has had relatively few converts from Islam. Almost all the conversions from Islam followed the political reconquest of the Iberian Peninsula and Sicily by Christian powers. Comparatively few converts have come from Buddhism, Hinduism, or Confucianism. Most of Christianity's territorial gains have been either by migration or by conversion from animism and polytheism. That is true even in Asia, the home of the high religions. The amazing geographic strides of Christianity in the past hundred and fifty years have been by migrations of previously "Christian" peoples, or among "primitive" folk in the Americas, the Pacific, Africa, and Asia. Christianity has won millions in China and hundreds of thousands in Japan from constituencies of advanced faiths, but these conversions have been largely from those whose confidence in the existing religions had already been shaken by the impact of Western civilization.

An explanation which appears more nearly to account for the facts is the close association of religion with culture. Each religion which long endures contributes to the formation of a culture. It is not the sole creative factor but it is one of them. Thus Islam has its culture, although that is compounded of many other and earlier elements. There is a Hindu civilization.

Buddhism carried with it to the lands to which it went much of the culture of the India in which it had arisen, yet modified by Buddhism and, in some of its art, by Greek contributions. It was never triumphant unless it could have dominance, as in Tibet, Burma, Siam, and, for a time, in Japan, and could be a major factor in shaping a culture. In China it never occupied this position. India is primarily Hindu and Hinduism is Indian. Chinese civilization was mainly Confucian. Judaism is a culture as well as a religion. There have been what have been called Christian civilizations. Manichaeism seems to have disappeared in part because it did not become identified with a major persistent culture. Taoism has been a minority force because it did not become dominant in China. It owes its long continued life in some degree to its association with certain strains in Chinese culture. As a culture with which a religion is associated declines, the religion itself also loses ground.

However, this hypothesis is far from fitting all the facts. Few if any cultures are identical with any religion. Certainly India does not fully embody the Hindu idea of *ahimsa,* harmlessness. Nor does any culture conform to the Buddhist regard for all living creatures. No civilization has ever adequately incorporated the ideals of Christ. Christianity, as we will point out more at length later, has not been identified with any culture. It has displayed a strange capacity for surviving the death of cultures with which it has been intimately associated and, freed from them, has gone on to fresh power. In this it has been unique.

Moreover, even if a complete correlation were established between a culture and a religion, we would still be far from answering our question. We would need to know why cultures rise and fall. Is it because of their failure fully to embody the ideals of a religion, or is it because of the weaknesses in the religion by which they have been profoundly influenced? Is Confucianism the cause of the long stagnation of China? Is a triumphant Islam the source of the sterility of much of the culture which bears its name? Is Western civilization ill because it has not really tried the Christianity which was long its professed faith? Or is its malady to be ascribed to the impossibility of the standards with which Christianity confronts it? Is it dying of maladjustment between its alleged ideal and its achievements, a maladjustment which was inherent in the contrast between the demands of Christianity and man's nature? Or are the deaths of cultures to be ascribed to other causes? We cannot as yet fully know.

That there is some correlation between the course of a culture and that of a religion with which it is associated is clear. It must also be obvious on careful examination that the correlation is by no means identity. In it is not to be found the full explanation of the rise and decay of religions.

There is a possible explanation which is based upon an interpretation of the Christian faith. It is not a necessary deduction from the Gospel. There can be others. Nor is it one that is usually given. It is here put forward purely as a hypothesis. As Christians we must believe that God has always been striving with man. God desires that no man should perish but that all should come to a knowledge of the truth. Yet He has given to man a limited measure of free will. He does not force His will on man. As, after the last ice age, civilization became more complex and urban cultures arose, man, in response to God's spirit, developed better insights into his own nature and destiny. Yet always those insights were clouded by sin. For some reason which we cannot now know, God found the least trammeled response in the small minority who constituted the Hebrew lawgivers and prophets and their followers. Through them He was able to prepare for the full revelation of Himself and work His redemption of man through Christ. This may account for the emergence of so many of the high religions at about the same time. Some of them interacted on one another, as did Hinduism and Buddhism, Judaism and Christianity, and Judaism and Christianity on the one hand and Islam on the other. Yet in their origin several of the great systems appear to have had no reciprocal connection. The usually accepted dates (although for the first two there is much doubt) make Zoroaster, the Buddha, and Confucius approximately contemporaries. However, there is not the slightest evidence that any one of them influenced the others or that they arose out of a common cultural urge. It looks as though God were seeking at the same time in various cultural areas to make Himself known.

Of all these religions Christianity is the only one which continues to expand in any major way. Of all of them it has suffered least from stagnation, decay, and loss of ground. It may well be that the reason is to be found in the unique nature of Christianity. What we call Christianity is the vehicle of the Gospel. It is not identical with the Gospel, but it is the chief means by which the Gospel is mediated to men. We are later to point out the fact that, in contrast with the other religions, Christianity has continued to gain in the total human scene. That may well find its reason in the fact that the Gospel is the gift of God and as such meets the basic and continuing needs of men as does none of its rivals. These others, with their imperfect insights and their errors, do not have the answer to man's hunger or contain the healing for his sickness. It is only through the Gospel that these are met and that man's true goal is to be found. As Augustine, after trying various other roads, so unmistakably found: "Thou hast made us for Thyself and our heart can find no rest until it rests in Thee." The other proffered ways pass, faulty and imperfect as they are, in their essence mixed

with man's pride and sin. The Gospel goes on, because, being
God's word to man, it alone speaks convincingly to his condition.

This does not necessarily mean that the Gospel is finally to
win the allegiance of all men. To that question we are to come
later. It does mean that it is both timely and timeless, that in
every age it is God's word to men and that so long as man is man
it is the power of God unto his salvation.

We are to see that, in contrast with the other religions, Christianity appears to be gaining as a factor in the life of mankind.
Unlike the others, which rise, flourish, and wane, as a force in
history it is in its youth. We are living in the early days of the
Church.

II

If Christianity is still young, then the forms which it has thus
far taken may not be necessarily its final or normal ones. The
Gospel is the eternal word of God to man. So far as we know,
man's nature and fundamental needs do not change. The Gospel
is God's way of meeting man's needs and bringing his nature to
its full fruition—likeness to God unmarred by sin. Christianity
is the garb or garbs in which the Gospel finds expression. It is
the product of man's response to the Gospel. It bears the impress
of particular environments, of the cultures in which the Gospel
has been planted. In its organization, its forms of worship, and
the intellectual formulations of its faith Christianity displays the
influence of the cultures into which the Gospel has gone. This
is inevitable. It is a phase of the Incarnation. The Word becomes flesh. It does so once for all in Jesus of Nazareth. But in a
sense Christ in reincarnated in each era and culture. He has his
living epistles. In each age there are those of whom it can be
said, with Paul: "It is no longer I who live, but Christ who lives

in me." Each incarnation has the stamp upon it of its milieu. That means that institutional and visible expressions of Christianity must change from culture to culture and from period to period. If a particular expression of Christianity does not adjust itself to meet the shifting environment, it languishes and eventually perishes.

If, in changing, Christianity does violence to the Gospel it also suffers. If in seeking to mediate the Gospel it accommodates itself fully to its setting, that particular form of it passes. If it is so conformed to this world that those who give it their allegiance are not transformed, eventually it becomes sterile.

This has happened again and again. In the early centuries Ebionism and Gnosticism went this way. The Ebionites were those who attempted to make Christianity a sect of Judaism. In doing so they carried over so much of the Jewish heritage that the Gospel was obscured. The Gnostics represented a climate of opinion, a method of thought which was widespread in the Mediterranean world of their day. They sought to express the Gospel in that pattern. In doing so they so badly distorted it that some of its essential elements were lost. As the environment changed, Christian Gnosticism died.

We are, however, in danger of going to the other extreme and of insisting that the forms of Christianity which have been handed down from the past are for all time the normal and final expressions of the Gospel. Because in their age and environment they have been successful incarnations of the Gospel we contend that they must always be such. As the environment and the culture change, they become more and more out of touch with it and are clung to by dwindling minorities.

Somewhere between these two extremes are the forms of Christianity which will become the main current by which the Gospel is transmitted. On the one hand, they must not be so nearly adjusted to their age and surroundings that they have sacrificed the essence of the Gospel. On the other hand, in seeking to safeguard the Gospel they must not cling so tenaciously to the institutions of an earlier age that they cramp the Gospel. They must not bind the Gospel in the graveclothes of the past. They must not seek to keep the always fresh ferment of the Gospel in the inflexible wineskins of a bygone age. If they do, it will suffer damage and, for many, be lost.

Because of our failure to obtain a true historical perspective, most of us are in danger of regarding as final the expressions of Christianity to which we have become accustomed or to mistake as essential and eternal the accidental features inherited from a past culture.

Every one of the forms of Christianity which exists is in part the product of a particular environment. This is true of all of the churches which we think of as Catholic. They are sprung from the Catholic Church which came into being in the Roman Empire. That church reflected in part the conditions and temper of that realm. Its episcopate and its dioceses were to some degree counterparts of the imperial administrative machinery. Its creeds arose out of the theological controversies of the day. Many of us recognize that these creeds state timeless truths and believe that had we been present when they were framed we would have sided with those who accepted them. Yet we must also be aware that these documents in their emphases echo the debates out of which they arose and use a terminology which requires explanation to those of another age. Thus the Apostles' Creed can be really understood only in connection with the Marcionites, whose special tenets it denied by positive affirmations. The Nicene symbol or formula reflects the Arian controversy. We may be able honestly to subscribe to the Apostles' and the Nicene Creed and be grateful for them, but we cannot think of them as well-rounded, balanced descriptions of the Gospel.

The several Eastern churches which dissented from this Catholic Church still carry the marks of the differences which led to their departure. Thus the Armenian or Gregorian Church is clearly the church of a particular nation and prospers or languishes with that nation. The Coptic Church is the remnant of an ancient Egyptian nationalism which has been superseded by a nationalism which centers about Islam. The Nestorians are pitiable survivors of a set of social patterns which have largely vanished.

The Orthodox fellowship of churches, a development from the Catholic Church of the Roman Empire, continues both the features of that church and the peculiarities which came to it because of the part of the Empire in which it developed. It was in that portion of the Empire where no collapse of the state occurred but where power became more and more centralized in the throne. It therefore inherited in part the tradition of its non-Christian predecessors which put religion under the control of the state. It tended to confine itself to worship and to world-denying monasticism, to divide into state churches, and to have no inclusive structure which embraced the whole. The Russian Orthodox Church, tied hand and foot to the state by Peter the Great, was the logical outcome. The Soviet regime has been ironically consistent with the historical tendency of the Orthodox Church when it first insisted that the Church confine itself to its "proper" function, the holding of religious services, and not seek to influence the social or economic order, and then, later, sought to make the church subserve the interests of Russian nationalism and imperialism in resistance to the Germans and in furthering Russian ambitions in Central Europe and the Balkans.

There is as much of fact as of fiction in the famous quip that the Roman Catholic Church is the ghost of the Roman Empire. To a high degree the Roman Catholic Church embodies the temper of that realm. There is a striking fitness in supplanting the imperial image on Trajan's pillar by a statue of Peter. Not only has the Fisherman seemed to triumph in Rome but Rome also has in part vanquished the Fisherman. The temper of the Roman Catholic Church is imperial. It is significant that the chief stronghold of that church has been in the section of Europe which was most thoroughly Romanized, namely, the present Italy, Spain, Portugal, France, and South Germany. As we are to suggest later, the weakening of this area by the wars of the present century is ominous for the future of the Roman Catholic Church. We need to recall, moreover, that the claim of the Roman Catholic Church to control all aspects of life issued in some degree from the collapse of much of Roman government in Italy and Western Europe and the fashion in which, in response to the need, that church stepped into the breach to defend the weak and the poor and to maintain order in a time of threatened anarchy. The activism of Western Christianity in contrast with the passive other-worldliness of the Orthodox Church arises to a certain extent from a difference of environment.

The great Anglican Communion is the Church of England. It has helped to mold the English temper and is in turn a reflection of that temper. Its combination of Catholic and Protestant elements is an element of its strength, but it springs from a particular set of policies followed deliberately for purposes of state, notably by Elizabeth.

Protestantism, we need again and again to remind ourselves, is the form of Christianity which arose in the northwest of Europe and the British Isles and in its main divisions reflects the political history of that region. Lutheranism is German and

Scandinavian. The Reformed churches were in large part the type of Christianity which prevailed in the border lands between the Latin South and the non-Latinized North. The surviving radical Protestant bodies, such as the Baptists, Congregationalists, Quakers, and Methodists, are chiefly of Anglo-Saxon growth and are characteristic of Anglo-Saxon Christianity, whether in the British Isles, the British Dominions, or the United States.

Since all forms of Christianity have developed in particular environments and have borne the earmarks of their milieu, none can be expected to endure unaltered.

Presumably the main stream of Christianity will go on through that branch which most combines flexibility and adaptability to new environments on the one hand, with loyalty in life and deed to the Gospel on the other.

This does not mean that the Christianity of the future, to persist, must ignore all the developments between the New Testament and its day. In some fashion the accumulated wealth of Christian experience must be transmitted. Each new form of Christianity arises from some predecessor. There is no complete break. Even protests against the corruption in the Church are, as protests, conditioned by the past against which they rebel. Ideally each new stage of Christianity must carry forward what earlier generations of Christians have learned of the richness of the Gospel.

From which of the existing forms of Christianity is the next advance chiefly to come? Is it one of the Eastern churches, the Roman Catholic Church, the Anglican Communion, or one or a group of the varied forms of Protestantism? The Christianity of the future will be continuous from one or more of the present branches. But will the proportionate strength of the several branches be the same as now or will it be different? From which will the main currents proceed?

III

This leads us to the third of the main issues with which we must concern ourselves in this book. What can and should we as Christians do to help guide the future course of Christianity?

Obviously the shaping of the future is by no means entirely in our hands. It is in large part determined by forces quite beyond our control. Environment which we can have no share in creating and the past which was there before our birth will be potent. Clearly, too, God is at work in the environment, in the past, and in the future. Christianity centers in the eternal Gospel, which is the gift of God.

However, quite as obviously, we can share in shaping the future of the faith. We are not automata. Much depends upon our response to the Gospel. We must seek to understand it and to give ourselves to it. We must inquire what it means for us and for those of our generation. We must ask what we can do to help make it effective in our age. What methods shall we employ? Shall we, as did the generation of Christians immediately behind us, aim at "the evangelization of the world in this generation"? Shall we plan for a widespread evangelism which shall seek the mass conversion of tribes and nations, even when we know, from past experience, that such a conversion will, for the majority, be superficial? Shall we endeavor to realize in the world immediately ahead of us a Christian civilization? We know that no civilization can be fully Christian in the sense of embodying completely the ideals of the Sermon on the Mount. But shall we strive to make world-wide what we have had in the Occident where Christianity has been a living force for many centuries? Shall we work for a civilization embracing all men where at least nominal allegiance shall be given to Christianity by the overwhelming majority, as was once the case in Western

Europe and where in theory the rightness or wrongness of an act, a custom, or an institution was judged by Christian standards? Shall we dream of permeating all phases of life everywhere by the spirit of Christ?

Or shall we content ourselves in the next stage ahead with being a minority? Christians have never been a majority. If the world be taken as a whole, that is true even of nominal Christians. Where, as in the Roman Empire from the fourth century onward and in much of Europe, all but a few of the population have been baptized as a social convention, groups arose which strove fully to embody the Christian ideal. Some of these were monastic. Some were sects which separated from the official church or were expelled from it. Shall we in the day ahead concentrate on building such "cells" of those who are completely committed to Christ? The world in which we live seems peculiarly hostile. Can we not best serve the coming generations by stressing the formation and multiplication of small groups which will seek fully in their individual and collective living to realize without compromise Christian standards? Such groups need not be world-denying in the sense of withdrawing from it completely and abandoning it to its fate. They can seek to influence it and serve it. But shall we stress the absolute attainment of the Christian life by a few, so far as that may be done in history, or try to bring all society to professed acceptance of the Gospel and thus to a much watered-down version of the Christian life?

How far shall we view with equanimity the departure of Christians from ecclesiastical patterns inherited from the past? Shall we insist upon adherence to the old and, if not, how far shall we encourage the emergence of new forms? How far can what we do or fail to do determine from which branch of Christianity the future is to stem? The strength and the weakness of Christianity in the days ahead may be in large part determined by the vision, the adaptability, and yet the basic loyalty of the adherents of the branch which by its nature and its present strength appears best fitted to be the main source of the Christianity of the future.

Most important of all is the question: How shall we tap the eternal springs of power? How shall we so lay ourselves open to the Spirit of God that He may use us to further His kingdom?

CHAPTER II

THE CURRENT THREAT AND CHALLENGE

THE very existence of Christianity seems threatened. Seldom if ever has the menace to Christianity been so grave as in the present century. Were one simply to fix his gaze on the adverse forces, he might come to the conclusion that Christianity, like other religions, has reached the peak of its career and is irretrievably declining as a vital force in the life of mankind.

Yet the world also presents Christianity with a challenge— a challenge not to survival but to advance and to fresh victories. The famous word in the New Testament pictures the Church not as a beleaguered city but as a besieging army, not as on the defensive but as attacking. "The powers of death shall not prevail against it."

Both the threat and the opportunity are familiar to all thoughtful observers. There is, however, an advantage in a study such as this of outlining them both and noting something of their nature.

I

First of all, we are living in the midst of vast revolutions. As never before in human history old customs are disintegrating. The familiar world is passing. A new world is struggling to be born.

It is significant for Christianity that these revolutions have their source in the Occident, in the very region where Christianity has had its traditional strength and has been longest at work. The revolutions are in large part, so we are accustomed to say, the outgrowth of science and of its product, the machine, and of new and radical ideas of the universe, of society, and of man. All have had their spring in the West, in Europe and the overseas extensions of Europe.

These forces have wrought the transformation of Europe, so that we speak of "the decline of the West." Clearly the old Occident is passing.

The revolutions have been even more catastrophic among non-Occidental peoples. There a double revolution has been in progress. One has followed the invasion of the culture of the aggressive West. The cultures of the peoples of Africa, of the Pacific Islands, of the American aborigines, and of the nations of Asia have been shaken and, in some instances, shattered, by the impact of the expanding Occident. Witness especially Japan, China, and Africa south of the Sahara. This revolution in itself would have been grave enough. But to that has been added another. The culture which has produced the revolution is itself in revolution. The changes in this invading culture are having their repercussions upon the cultures upon which it is impinging. The result has been even greater disintegration among some non-Occidental lands than in the Occident.

These conditions have been both a menace and an appeal to Christianity. They have obviously been a menace. Christianity has built itself into the life of the Occident. Indeed, that life to some degree has been its creation. Christianity has, therefore, become intimately associated with the existing order. Since that order is passing, Christianity might also be expected to pass with it. In Russia, for example, the Orthodox Church was closely knit with the Czarist regime. The Communists naturally regarded it as part of the structure which they were resolved to sweep aside. The church suffered. This is not surprising. What is amazing are the vitality and survival of the church.

Yet the revolutions have also been an appeal. In the Occident they have presented Christianity with a new order in which, if it is to be true to its genius, it must endeavor to persist and grow. In non-Occidental lands the disintegration of the old cultures has removed a major resistance to Christianity and has made it possible for that faith to spread as never before. When they were intact, the old cultures presented an almost solid front against the entrance of Christianity. Now they, together with their resistance, are passing. New cultures are in the making and Christians, if they are alert to their opportunity, can weave the Gospel into their texture. To be sure, old antagonisms have not fully disappeared and new ones have entered. Islam, Hinduism, and Buddhism are still resistant. In many lands nationalism and Communism offer enhanced opposition. Yet the challenge is there.

II

One of the most obvious aspects of the revolutions is the ideologies associated with some of them. Of these Communism is currently the most aggressive, but they have recently included Fascism and National Socialism. As we have been reminded again and again, these are rivals of the historic religions. They have demanded the undivided allegiance of their adherents. They may tolerate religion, but they do so grudgingly. Russian Communism has frankly proclaimed that religion is the opiate of the people. These ideologies had their rise in what were once known as Christian lands and their antireligious operations have been directed more against Christianity than against any other faith. To be sure, National Socialism was peculiarly bitter against the Jews, but that was primarily against the Jews as a race and only incidentally against Judaism as a religion.

Fascism and National Socialism have been overthrown in stern war, but Communism, associated with Russian nationalism and imperialism, is more powerful than ever. It is the twentieth-century equivalent of Islam. Thirteen centuries ago the latter, inspiring the Arabs and borne by them, much as Communism and the Russians are related, tore about half its territory from Christianity. Most of that territory is still held by Islam. Christianity has been able to regain only some of its periphery, notably the Iberian Peninsula. Communism appears to constitute a similar threat. Like Islam, it is younger than Christianity, comes fresh into the world, and early in its course has had the prestige of great military victories. As was true of Islam in the latter's youthful days, its weaknesses have not yet become fully apparent.

Socialism in the forms in which it is known in the British Isles, Western Europe, and the United States is less palpably a rival of Christianity. Yet it holds the exclusive loyalty of many of its advocates and has, for them, eliminated Christianity.

III

Certain world-wide aspects of the revolutions, broader than any one of the new ideologies, present grave threats. One of these is the growing power of the state. In the twentieth century the state is assuming more and more functions which once belonged to the Church. Among these the chief is education, with the shaping of the oncoming generations.

This is not the first age in which the state has been a menace to the Church. At the very outset the Roman Empire threatened it and persecuted it. In the sixteenth and seventeenth centuries the absolute monarchies of Europe endeavored to control it.

This was true not only of the Tudor and Stuart kings in England and of the Protestant princes of Scandinavia and Germany, but also of the Roman Catholic kings of Spain, Portugal, and France and of the Orthodox Russian Czars. Yet these rulers, professedly Christian, did not take its functions from the Church: they simply sought to control it, to operate through it, and to make it serve their interests. The Church still had in its hands the training of youth and the care of the sick and the poor. In our day some of the totalitarian states have been hostile to the Church and have been determined to deprive it of the education of youth and of all its social functions. The more extreme have prohibited the teaching of the Christian faith to youth and have, instead, indoctrinated them with their own ideologies. This has been notably true of the Communist Soviets. To a slightly less degree it was true of the Nazis. The Fascists had a similar purpose but found the Roman Catholic Church so strong in Italy that they had to compromise with it. In Turkey the government has sought to subordinate religion to nationalism.

Even some governments which are not palpably hostile to Christianity and in some respects are friendly have partly crowded the Church out of education. This is the case in the United States. The system of state schools enrolls the overwhelming majority of the youth. The state schools must be "neutral" in religion. This is largely because of the differing convictions held by the citizens and the impossibility of teaching one form of religion without antagonizing the adherents of other forms. Yet the net result is to push the teaching of religion out of the regular system of schools and to leave it to Sunday schools or to forms of weekday religious instruction which find it difficult to obtain the attention of more than a minority of the youth. Most of the hospitals and other institutions for the suffering and underprivileged are also supported by the state and Christianity in any of its formal expressions is usually omitted.

In almost every land the twentieth-century stress on nationalism tends to put loyalty to the state above loyalty to God. The hard lot of pacifists, even those who are pacifists on Christain grounds in nominally Christian lands, is witness to this condition. Until recently no alien who put fidelity to God above allegiance to the state could be naturalized in the United States—a position which made it impossible for an intelligent, consistent Christian to become a citizen.

In Japan until the defeat of that country Christians had difficulty in maintaining their faith against the demands of state Shinto. In India the trend of nationalism is to prohibit all change of religion, including the acceptance of Christianity. In some Moslem lands the state makes conversion to Christianity so difficult as to be almost impossible.

The trend of the times is for the state to assume more, not fewer, functions. Christianity will, therefore, find the state a more and not a less difficult rival.

In this enhanced role of the state are more subtle dangers. They are the inclination to leave all functions to the state and to make Christianity ancillary.

In the nineteenth century American and many British Christians were accustomed to depending upon nongovernmental initiative and agencies. In this atmosphere the voluntary support of churches and of church enterprises thrived. Today we expect the state to care for various phases of human needs. To meet these tasks taxes have mounted and have cut into the sources of gifts to churches. The trend is away from private and Church responsibility.

Moreover, religion and, with it, Christianity are regarded as useful in so far as they make for the prosperity of government.

Christianity is commended because it furthers democracy. The public is exhorted to support Christianity because it makes for law, order, and the welfare of society as embodied in the state. Even some apologists for Christianity argue that the faith supports government. It is true that Christianity has historically been the chief root of the democratic ideal and that the sense of moral responsibility which it engenders is essential to the successful operation of democracy. But to value it for this utilitarian motive, however worthy, is to denature Christianity. Christianity, if it is true to its genius, places first not the state but God. The early Christians insisted that if it came to a choice they must serve God rather than men. The martyrdoms of the first centuries were largely on this issue. The Christians declined to participate in the imperial cult, a symbol of loyalty to the state, and were, accordingly, regarded as anarchists. The Christian must give primary place to the will of God, even if this leads him to disobey the government. The trend, then, to praise Christianity because of its political utility, especially for the democracies, is perilous. Because the issue is not so obvious as in the opposition of totalitarian states based on palpably anti-Christian ideologies, the threat to Christianity may be even greater.

Yet in this menace of the state a challenge is presented for which Christianity may be the stronger. When the opposition is open and the Church is feared as an enemy and not used as a tool, the native antagonism between the Gospel and the world is revealed in all its starkness. The greater peril is "when all men speak well" of Christianity and when the Church is popular and is employed as an instrument for maintaining the existing order. In the persecution which ensues when the antimony is recognized, the Church may be kept to a minority. Sometimes, as in the Moslem lands of the Near East or as in the ancient Syrian Church in India, it may remain an encysted minority, progressively sterile in its inner life and with little or no influence on its environment. It may even be strangled and completely vanish. But, if the persecution is not too intense and persistent and the inner loyalty to the Gospel is sufficiently strong, the Church, even though a small minority, may be more vital than when it is more popular. This, for instance, was the case with the Moravians. A remnant from the devastation of the Thirty Years' War, in the quiet of Herrnhut and fusing with the contributions of Pietism, they were a minority but contributed mightily to the great awakenings in Europe, Great Britain, and America of the eighteenth and nineteenth centuries.

The peril presented by those who would take from the Church the shaping of youth may starve the Church. It may also impel the Church to new and better ways of reaching youth and result in a more intelligent, loyal commitment, even though that may be only by a few.

The more subtle menace presented by the attitude which values Christianity chiefly as an aid to democracy may, if Christians are alert, serve to point out even more sharply the true nature of the Gospel, the fact that the Gospel can never be fully at home in any general political or social order, that it must always protest as well as heal and inspire, and that to make God the tool of any form of government which mankind devises is blasphemy.

IV

Many have regarded as another of the products of the Occident which is incompatible with Christianity science and the scientific attitude. That need not be so. Indeed, the quantity of writing on that issue is so enormous and the Christian faith of so many men of undoubted scientific competence is so well-established that we here need not go into the issue.

However, what to many has seemed the contradiction has been a menace to Christianity. That was true throughout much of the nineteenth century. It has been also the case in the twentieth century. How many have given up their faith, have had it weakened, or have been prevented from becoming Christians by the supposed irreconcilability of science and Christianity we will never know, but the total has undoubtedly run into the millions. The threat has been notable in the Occident. It has also been important in non-Occidental lands, especially among the intellectuals. In the march of knowledge in some areas the necessary adaptation of the intellectual statement of Christian faith has not quickly been made. That adaptation has been achieved by a few, but their conclusions have not penetrated the rank and file of Christians at a pace which has kept up with scientific advance. Even in university circles in lands long under Christian influence little awareness exists of the recent conclusions of Christian thought. Because of the pressure upon them to keep abreast of their own field of specialization, many scholars are abysmally ignorant of Christian scholarship. They ignore or denounce what they believe to be Christianity when they are religiously little better than illiterates and what they scorn is not held by well-informed Christians. Their attitude has been infectious and has spread widely among university graduates. It characterizes, too, much of the public.

The threat has been heightened by those who in the name of Christianity have rejected well-established conclusions of science. Many who in childhood or early youth have been under the tutelage of those who have denounced the findings of science have come in adolescence or late youth to question these assertions and in doing so have felt that they could no longer consistently remain Christians.

Yet the challenge of science has compelled Christians to rethink their faith. It has led them to be impatient with the routine reiteration of old formulas simply because they are venerable. It has driven them to ask again the old questions, but in new language, and to state in fresh vocabulary the eternal Gospel. In doing so many have come to see that the ancient creeds are efforts to put into language continuing truth, but they have been made ill content with a second-hand religion and have been driven to find its living springs for themselves and their fellows. The validity and power of the Gospel are such that where men, no matter of what era or from what climate of opinion, open their hearts to them, they will learn anew the marvelous transforming force there revealed. If Christianity did not have in it the Gospel, the eternal word of God, it would perish, but because the Gospel is "the power of God for salvation to every one who has faith," no matter of what period or culture or race, every threat by the channel of the intellect can be a stimulus to a fresh outpouring of its redemptive power.

v

Closely allied to the scientific approach and also strong in what was until recently regarded as Christendom are several varieties of nontheistic humanism. These profess to give great dignity to man and to make unnecessary the Gospel of divine revelation and salvation. They may and often do honor Jesus as a great figure whose ethical teachings help man in his long struggle from the brute. They believe that the religious aspects of Jesus' teaching are not essential to his morals or his ideal of man. They may even claim to preserve religion, but religion as they define it is far from what is meant by Christianity.

We need not here demonstrate the weakness or, compared with the Christian view of man, the shallowness, poverty, and futility of these kinds of humanism. That is not our task. It has been performed elsewhere. We must point out that this humanism has its roots partially in Christianity. Historically the possibilities which it holds out to man have to no small degree sprung from Christian rootage. It is from the high dignity which the Gospel gives to redeemed human beings that much of contemporary humanistic value is derived. We must also recall that in our Lord's teachings God is central, that the children of the kingdom are called to be perfect as their heavenly Father is perfect, and that the command to love one's neighbor as oneself is seen to be a corollary of the command to give complete devotion and love to God. It is because men, redeemed, saved, are embarked upon the everlasting life which consists in knowledge of God as revealed in Christ and of eternal fellowship with Him that the Gospel is the source of such astounding possibilities for man. To leave out this belief in the God and Father of our Lord Jesus Christ is to rob that conviction of its foundation.

However, for many for whom belief in God is difficult nontheistic humanisms are appealing. They seem to find support in evolution. The geologists assure us that the course of life on this planet has been from lower to higher forms. They point out the development and disappearance of many lower forms. They insist that the course of evolution has favored the being, man, who has shown the greatest intelligence. They hopefully declare that, geologically speaking, man is still young. They predict for him a long and glorious future. Much in this is appealing and is not inconsistent with Christian faith. Some earnest and devout Christians who are also scientists of repute hold to it. It can, however, be so taught as to seem to make God and redemption unnecessary.

The tragedies of the present century have dealt optimistic nontheistic humanism severe blows. Man has been seen to be capable of individual and collective baseness and degeneracy on a colossal scale. If individuals have displayed great heroism and high, unselfish devotion and have shown what man may become, it is also apparent that man may destroy civilization and fall into a state that is worse than barbarism. The automatic progress of mankind through evolution of which so much was made by nineteenth-century optimists is seen to be a will-o'-the-wisp.

Yet many, belated, cling to nontheistic humanism. They whistle to keep up their courage or ignore unpleasant facts which might disillusion them. Thousands of them are still left in the United States, for as yet that land is not so seriously affected by the perils of the age as are some other parts of the world. The Communist or near-Communist and the socialist forms of nontheistic humanism win the allegiance of many who feel that somewhere there must be salvation from mankind's ills and scornfully or wistfully despair of finding it elsewhere.

Here, too, Christians have an opportunity. They can point out the weaknesses of nontheistic humanisms and show how far beyond these schools of thought is the Christian view and hope of man. They can show that the Christian conviction is more realistic in its recognition of the depravity of man and that the destiny it reveals of the goal of redeemed man is far higher than that of its humanistic rivals. By their lives they can demonstrate that their hope is not a vain myth.

VI

Nearly related to nontheistic humanisms is what may be termed secularism. It does not express itself in as well-articulated intellectual systems of thought as does humanism. It is akin to humanism in that its goals are purely this-worldly. It insists in

..tice that the main goals of life are not to be obtained through the Christian faith or, indeed, through any religion. It is absorbed in achieving food, clothing, and shelter, in improving what it terms "the standard of living." If it makes room for religion at all, it is merely as a means of attaining this goal. In its broader aspects it can be cultured and charming. It values art, music, literature, good manners, and the many amenities. It scorns what is crude. It wishes men to live as "civilized" beings. Yet it denies, either in theory or practice or both, any life beyond the grave. It insists on having its pie here instead of waiting for it in a "heaven bye-and-bye." It values prestige and wealth.

Secularism is by no means new. It is as old as civilization. Its goals are those which many pagans have long sought. It has been a persistent and constant menace to the Gospel and again and again has penetrated and corrupted Christianity. In the course of the centuries many thousands have accepted the Christian name because they believed that by doing so they would be better provided with food and shelter. Centuries ago the Frisians listened respectfully to the preaching of Wilfrid of York because during the winter he was with them the catch of fish on which they heavily relied for a livelihood was better than normal. Not only in our Lord's time but also in all ages since there have been those who have sought him because they believed that through him they ate their fill of the loaves.

Secularism is peculiarly dangerous because the petition for daily bread imbedded in the Lord's Prayer seems to favor it and because Christians are charged to feed the hungry and clothe the naked. The this-worldy values of the Gospel are obvious. Christianity makes for industry, thrift, and cleanliness. Even monastic communities which by their rules deny property to their individual members become collectively wealthy. All too often prosperity has been deemed evidence of piety.

The menace of secularism, ever present, has been accentuated in the nineteenth and twentieth centuries by at least two factors. One has been the development of the machine and the great increase in wealth issuing from it. The machine has produced goods far beyond the wildest imaginings of earlier generations. It has made possible for millions what were once luxuries for the very few and has opened to all physical comforts which were unknown to princes not many generations ago. Contrast the palace at Versailles and its lack of plumbing and of toilet and bathing facilities with what is deemed essential for even modest American and British homes of our day. Because these goods which mean comfort are so obtainable, men bend their energies toward their acquisition. Men are preoccupied with "security," by which they mean assured food, clothing, and shelter on a scale made feasible by the machine, to a greater degree than when the physical miseries made them painfully aware that this world is "a wilderness of woe," "this world is not" their "home." This is not, of course, to advocate a return to involuntary poverty or to decry the efforts of Christians who strive through many channels to feed the hungry and clothe the naked and to make possible a higher physical standard of comfort for all. It is a matter of emphasis. Yet the accessibility of wealth through the machine has for many brought near "the deceitfulness of riches."

The threat of secularism has been augmented by the current intellectual skepticism of religious values. That skepticism is due to the many causes which we have already outlined. Strong and mounting in the last hundred years or so, it has contributed mightily to man's agelong secularism.

One of the perils associated with secularism is the ease with which institutions bearing the Christian name and springing from a Christian source become secularized. In stressing the undoubted values of Christianity in producing character which is honest, industrious, and public-spirited some churches and related institutions tend to succumb to the atmosphere about them and to make character and this-worldly goals their only objectives. Christ is constrained to serve Mammon, but in so alluring a guise that the misdirection of energy is not clearly recognized until it has gone so far that it is reversed with difficulty.

The challenge, and hard it is to meet, is to make Christianity contribute to such this-worldly ends as are clearly demanded by its genius—among them peace, the relief of physical suffering, and the prevention of poverty—but to do so in such fashion that the eternal goal of the Gospel is not only not lost sight of but stressed. That this can be done is proved in the lives of our contemporaries. Many of those who have labored most diligently and effectively to improve the international situation and have been foremost as pioneers in the warfare against physical suffering have been inspired and sustained by their fellowship with God and their faith in the eternal verities. Some have led in the achievement of both the this-worldly and the other-worldly goals of the Gospel.

VII

The present century has seen vast dislocations of population which have made the task of the churches more difficult.

Some of these shifts have been in time of peace. The great cities which have grown from the industrialization of so much of the world have attracted millions who have thus been uprooted from their accustomed community associations. Among these associations have been the churches. The churches have made valiant efforts to reach the urban centers and not without success. Yet in the aggregate millions whose ancestors had church affiliations are now without them.

A phase of the threat through urbanization has been the loss to Christianity of much of the labor engaged in industry. This has been seen in most places where industrialization has gone far and the factory or the mining city has assumed large proportions. Sometimes, as in Roman Catholic circles in Europe, labor organizations connected with the Church have partly offset the trend, but the drift has been away from organized Christianity and from the faith itself.

The threat of urbanization to religion is not confined to Christianity. It is seen in most modern cities, whether in the Occident or in the Orient. As long as twenty-five years ago a survey in Tokyo showed the drift away from religious observances of the laborers in the factories. Country-born and bred as most of them were, when they moved to Tokyo and became employed in the mills they tended to drop the religious customs which had been theirs.

The dislocation of populations has been vastly augmented by the wars of the present century, especially by World War II. Millions have changed their homes to go into war industries. Other millions have been forcibly uprooted by invasions or deportations, whether in Europe or in Asia. Again the traditional community affiliations have been broken, and with them the connection with the Church.

These shifts of population constitute a challenge, but thus far Christianity has not caught up with it.

VIII

The wars of the present century have been an enemy of Christianity. Since they have centered in traditional Christendom and have been peculiarly devastating, they have proved an especially serious menace.

War is destructive of the moral principles which are among

the distinctive fruits of the Gospel. It makes for hatred, not love, for lying, not the truth, for killing, and not the saving of life. The sex standards upheld by Christianity are weakened by it. To be sure, heroism is there and loyalty and self-sacrifice on behalf of one's comrades. Yet the trend of war is distinctly against Christianity.

Then, too, the physical devastation of war brings difficulties for the churches. Church buildings are destroyed. Possible candidates for the clergy are deflected into war service and theological education suffers.

Moreover, in spite of the efforts of chaplains, millions in the armed services have less touch with religion than in peacetime. Millions of civilians have their energies so absorbed in munitions factories, war gardens, and home defense projects that they permit attendance at church services to slip.

The habit and system of war present a challenge to Christianity, not so much because of what war does to Christianity as because of what it does to mankind. Christian faith and conscience have not supinely accepted war. Evidence of this is the fact that international law, the League of Nations, and the United Nations arose within Christendom and in part from Christian rootage. Yet the trend of the twentieth century is clearly more destructive than constructive. Christianity has lost more from war than it has gained.

IX

Revolt against white imperialism also carries problems for Christianity.

In the past four and a half centuries the geographic spread of Christianity has been largely in connection with the expansion of European peoples. For the first three centuries of that time Christian missions, whether Russian Orthodox, Roman Catholic, or, with some notable exceptions, Protestant, were largely financed and directed by governments or official agencies such as the Dutch East India Company, and as part of the general colonial policy. For instance, in Spanish America the mission was the characteristic method employed by the state for the advance of the frontier. The California missions were planted largely for the purpose of countering Russian advance from the north and the Texas missions to offset the French. To be sure, missionaries often, indeed, usually, opposed the more ruthless aspects of imperialism and were protectors of the natives against rapacious conquerors and exploiters. Yet they worked in close conjunction with the colonial authorities.

In the nineteenth and twentieth centuries missions have been almost entirely without state support. They have sprung from voluntary agencies connected with the Church. Yet they have usually operated in areas which were being penetrated by white merchants and governments. In doing so they have sought to make the coming of the Occident a blessing and not a curse. Yet the current, although usually false accusation was that they were a phase of white imperialism.

During the present century we have seen a rapidly mounting tide of resentment against domination by the Occident. It is a feeling with which Christians can and should sympathize. Yet some of it is directed against missions and so offers an obstacle to Christianity in much of the non-Occidental world. It is seen in South Africa where the specious generalization is made that before the coming of the missionary the white man had the Bible and the blacks had the land, but that now the black man has the Bible and the white man has the land. From time to time, in such widely separated lands as Japan, China, Java, and Turkey, we have witnessed movements against Christianity on the ground that it was a part of white imperialism.

Obviously the challenge has also meant opportunity. It has facilitated the development of indigenous leadership and of indigenous initiative and self-support. It has hastened the rooting of Christianity among more peoples, so that the faith, as we are to see later, is much less exclusively identified with the Occident than it was at the dawn of the present century. Yet it also carries its threat.

x

The territorial advance of the great historic religions is not a serious part of the Christian problem. These faiths still offer resistance to the spread of Christianity. This is notably true of Islam, Hinduism, and, in some lands, Buddhism. Yet almost nowhere are any of these religions making such striking gains as to constitute an important threat to Christianity. To be sure, we still hear of the race between Christianity and Islam for the allegiance of parts of Africa and the East Indies, but not nearly so much as we did a generation or so ago. The chief dangers to Christianity are not here, but elsewhere.

This is significant. From one standpoint it might seem ominous. The major religions which mankind has known are on the defensive, stagnant, or moribund. If Christianity is of their company the outlook for it is grim.

From another standpoint the somnolence of the other great faiths holds in it both hope and challenge. As they become quiescent or die, the vacuum that they leave brings an added hunger and an additional need which Christianity can fill. The newer ideologies which compete for the successorship are inadequate. They are aggressive and at first appealing, but they cannot satisfy the deepest longings of the human spirit. Herein lie the opportunity for the Gospel and a great obligation upon Christians.

XI

A sobering feature of the current scene is the unpleasant fact that most of the outstanding new threats to Christianity, and, indeed, to all of the historic religions, have had their origin and chief centers of infection in the Occident. This is what we have learned to call Christendom, the area in which Christianity has been longest and most powerfully in operation. That is true whether the threat be the revolutions, the new ideologies, the growing power of the state, the scientific approach, the non-theistic humanisms, secularism, the dislocations of population, or war.

Does this mean that Christianity is self-destructive? Some of these forces—such as the new ideas which underlie and inspire the revolutions, the scientific approach, humanism, and the industrialism based upon science which is responsible for the accentuation of secularism and some of the shifts of population —can be traced in part to impulses which stem from Christianity. Marxist Communism arose from Hegelianism, and Hegel regarded himself as a Christian. Many of the early socialists were sincere Christians. Science in some degree springs from the confidence in the orderliness and dependability of the universe which was built into the European mind by the Christian faith of the medieval schoolmen and of men like Roger Bacon and Isaac Newton. Humanism, as we have seen, cherishes values which historically have come in largely from Christianity. Does Christianity, therefore, dig its own grave? By the very hopes and ideas which it inspires does it prepare the way for its own demise?

Obviously these threats to Christianity arise from perversions of the Gospel. But is there that in Christianity which lends itself to perversion?

In the nineteenth century apologists for Christianity ascribed to that faith the advances in Occidental civilization and saw in the contributions of science a proof of the superiority of Christianity over other religions. Now that it is apparent that mankind, through this very science, may hurtle into a condition worse than barbarism these voices are silent. Science is, of course, morally neutral. It may be used for man's well-being. It may be employed for man's infinite harm. If Christianity shares in the responsibility for science and hence in the achievements of science, must it not also acknowledge part of the responsibility not only for the beneficent but also for the destructive applications of science?

It looks as though this is the risk which God takes. He gives Himself to man in His Son and the Gospel. He accords to man enough of free will to twist even these supreme gifts to man's hurt. This is part of the human tragedy. Man is so made that he can misdirect even the grace of God.

Yet here, too, the story is not the seemingly simple one of decay. Redemption is at work. God's ways are not man's ways. God's word will not return to Him void but will accomplish that which He pleases and will prosper in the thing whereto He sent it. Of this we are to see evidence as our analysis progresses.

One description of the present situation would support the hypothesis that Christianity, like the other great religious systems of mankind, is passing. It would declare that the amazing spread of Christianity in the past four and a half centuries has been in connection with forces which basically are inimical to the Gospel —the passion for wealth and power—and that this expansion of the faith is not due to the inner vitality of Christianity but to the vigor of the peoples who have professed to accept it. It sees within what was once Christendom movements, partly arising from Christianity, which are hastening the disintegration not only of Christianity but also of all the other great historic faiths.

This hypothesis has much which seems to support it. We must not dodge it, unpalatable though it is. We shall see reasons for the conviction that it does not take account of all the facts. In these facts is ground, not for despair, but for great hope. In the combination of the facts which underlie the hypothesis and in the facts which invalidate the hypothesis is a way to a deeper insight into the human drama and its meaning.

CHAPTER III

THE LONG PERSPECTIVE

CHRISTIANITY has displayed an amazing ability to survive the death of cultures with which it has been intimately associated and to go on to fresh power in the life of mankind. Cultures rise and fall. Christianity modifies their course and may retard or hasten their demise. It never saves any culture from ultimate death. In some places and at some times it also disappears. In some other regions, with a change in the cultural scene, it persists, but sadly weakened. Yet on other occasions it not only survives, but it also salvages much of value from the perishing culture, transmits it to future generations, and itself displays renewed vigor. Indeed, the demise of a culture by which it has been bound sometimes frees Christianity for a greater display of its true nature and of its inherent power. Viewed against the background of the entire world, it goes forward by great pulsations. Each major period of crisis and decline is followed by another of advance. When mankind is seen as a whole, the influence of Christianity upon it becomes, in the course of these pulsations, progressively more extensive.

Not always does the same form of the faith carry on. The kind of Christianity which leads in the advance differs from age to age. It is more nearly accurate to say that Christianity often moves forward on more than one geographic front and through more than one of its organizational manifestations. The proportionate gains of the several churches vary. Some churches which once expanded widely dwindle or disappear. Some new forms of Christianity emerge and become prominent in the spread of the faith.

Yet through all the onward march certain convictions and features of the faith persist. The Christianity of the twentieth century differs from that of the first century, but the identities are greater than the contrasts.

It is to this story, so briefly summarized, that we are to give a slightly greater elaboration in this chapter. Even this amplification must still be a severe condensation. It affords reason, however, for the conviction that Christianity will outlive the threats of the present age and that by the crisis it will be emancipated from some of the handicaps imposed on it by its association with modern Western civilization and be enabled to show more of its true genius. The forms through which it will go on will not be in the same proportionate strength that we now know, but always what carries forward will be clearly Christianity and not another faith.

In all this story Christianity is unique among the religions of mankind. Unlike the others, it does not die. Not only, phoenixlike, does it come out of the fire with renewed life, but it also plays a larger and larger part in the affairs of men.

Let us, then, go on to make these generalizations more concrete by a rapid survey of the course of Christianity. Readers of the author's "A History of the Expansion of Christianity" series and *The Unquenchable Light* will find that the next few pages cover familiar ground. The repetition, however, is necessary if we are to acquire perspective for an interpretation of the present and a look ahead.

I

The first great period of the expansion of Christianity embraced its initial half millennium. Beginning as one of several obscure Jewish sects, and with many competitors who seemed to have a great advantage over it, within five centuries Christianity won the professed allegiance of the overwhelming majority of the population of the Roman Empire.

In doing so Christianity became closely associated with Graeco-Roman culture. It partly conformed to the intellectual patterns of the Graeco-Roman world: that is to say, it thought through and stated the Christian message in terms which to some extent were derived from Graeco-Roman philosophy. In phases of its devotional life it carried the impress of Neoplatonism. Its organization reflected that of the Empire. By no means did it become identical with its environment. It remained unique and was not fully "conformed to this world," but the affiliation with a particular culture was very close.

Through this association with Graeco-Roman culture, Christianity has continued to be largely integrated with one of the successors of that culture, the Occident. It has profoundly affected Western civilization. The latter, as distinct from another heir of the Graeco-Roman world, Islamic culture, is to a considerable degree the product of Christianity.

Not far from the time that Christianity seemed to triumph, the Roman Empire began palpably to disintegrate and traditional Graeco-Roman culture to break up.

Christianity was not the cause of this disaster. The coincidence seemed to many then and has seemed to some since to prove that Christianity was responsible. Augustine wrote his *City of God* to refute the charge. But before Christianity had assumed major numerical dimensions sterility had begun to be seen in the culture in which it was growing and decay had set in.

However, while it did not bring about the demise of Graeco-Roman civilization, Christianity did not prevent it. One of the early apologists declared in words that are much quoted in our day that Christians held the world together. In a larger sense than he dreamed his statement was confirmed by later developments, but Christians did not hold together the world that this apologist knew.

Yet Christianity not only survived the Roman Empire. It also arose to the challenge presented by the collapse and carried over to the next age some of the best features of the culture which had passed. Indeed, it became a more vigorous force in the succeeding culture in Western Europe than it would have been had the old structure persisted.

The contributions carried over by the Church from the ancient to the medieval world of Western Europe are well known. Most of the literature and learning which survived and much of the Roman law which the Middle Ages knew came through that source. The more intangible and no less important Roman temper endured because it was embodied in the Roman Catholic Church.

Well known, too, is the fashion in which the Church tutored the barbarians of Europe. She was their chief schoolmaster in civilization, in morals, and in high ideals. That she did not fully accomplish her task is evidenced in the Europe of today, with its thinly veiled barbarism and, here and there, its open reversion to paganism. Yet to such success as she had must be ascribed much, indeed the larger part of such culture as medieval Western Europe possessed.

What is not often recognized is the fashion in which Christianity, in rising to the emergency, displayed latent resources which would not otherwise have been evoked and became a greater factor in Western Europe than it would have been had the Empire persisted, unabated. This fact becomes apparent in the contrast between the eastern and the western portions of the north shore of the Mediterranean. In the former the Roman

Empire continued and the state controlled the Church. The Church developed elaborate and ornate services and the monasteries specialized on the interior life. The Church was not as subservient to the state as had been the pre-Christian official cults, yet it was cramped in giving full expression to the Christian faith. In the West, on the other hand, the disintegration of the Empire challenged the Church to the maintenance of an orderly society. The Church displayed sufficient vitality to rise to the need and took over many of the functions of the state. She provided Western Europe with its only inclusive structure, one which comprehended much more territory in that region than had the Roman Empire or than did the latter's alleged successor, the Holy Roman Empire. The Church of the West reached out into more areas of life than did its Eastern sister and permeated more aspects of the collective life of the West than did the Church of the East.

In this contrast is possibly to be found the greater creativity and abounding life of Western Europe. In the Byzantine realms the old structure of the Roman Empire went on, pursuing the autocratic and bureaucratic development which had begun before the professed conversion of the realm. Chistianity modified many of the aspects of life and enriched some of them—for instance, law, art, and architecture. The Eastern Church won the barbarians in the Balkans and Russia and tutored them in civilization. Yet through it Christianity did not give rise to such vigorous thought as it did through the Church of the West in the schoolmen and theology, or in education as did the Western Church in the monastic and cathedral schools and the universities, or in law as in the West through canon law, or in public morals as in chivalry, the Truce of God, the Peace of God, and, later, international law, all of them Western phenomena. These examples could be multiplied. Possibly, too, the more powerful currents of religious life in Western Europe, the richer development of the monastic system in Cluny, the Cistercians, the Franciscans, the Dominicans, the Waldensees, and the Lollards, to mention only a few and, later, the Protestant and Catholic Reformations, are to be ascribed to the fashion in which the collapse in the West brought out the latent powers of Christianity.

From the sixth to the thirteenth century Christianity, in its Nestorian form, spread across Asia. It did that in spite of the fact that it was a minority faith and was faced with persecuting cults backed by official support, first Zoroastrianism and then Islam.

On the other hand, in the thousand years which succeeded the slow breakup of the Roman Empire, in some vast areas Christianity lost ground which it has never regained. Islam gradually strangled the ancient churches on the northern shores of Africa and in Western and Central Asia. Indeed, that retreat has been continued in the present century, not fully offset by missions from the churches of the West. Nestorian Christianity died out in Chinese Turkestan, Mongolia, and China. The blood of the martyrs is not always the seed of the Church.

In spite of grave losses, however, by A.D. 1350 Christianity was a greater force in the life of mankind than it had been before the reverses which followed the collapse of the culture in which had been the first victories of the faith. Most of Europe was now ostensibly Christian—in contrast with the southern fringe (which had been Christian in A.D. 500). In that Europe cultures had arisen in which Christianity had been a more potent formative factor than it had been in the Graeco-Roman world, even in the later years of the Roman Empire. Christianity, too, was more widely extended. It was not so exclusively identified with the Mediterranean. Christian communities were to be found from Greenland and Iceland on the west and north to China on the east and the Sudan on the south.

II

Then came another transition which was dismaying and which threatened the very existence of Christianity. In Western Europe the culture which Christianity had more nearly shaped than it had any other gradually disintegrated. The Renaissance came, bringing in the South a thinly veiled revival of paganism. In the West the official church was divided and corrupt. Feudalism decayed and with it much of the economic and political organization on which the Church had rested. The Holy Roman Empire continued in theory, but in actuality was only a shadow and a memory. The all-embracing Church of which it was the spiritual counterpart was weakened. New absolute monarchies made the Church their servant and seemed to tie her to their chariot wheels. The advance of the Ottoman Turks brought a fresh forward surge of Islam which submerged Constantinople, long the eastern citadel of Christianity. The Christian minorities scattered across Central and Eastern Asia vanished. Voyages, discoveries, and conquests carried European peoples to the Americas, to the shores of Africa, to South and East Asia, and across Siberia. A weakened Christianity was confronted with an opportunity for expansion and a challenge to curb the atrocities of the *conquistadores* which in its palsied and divided state it seemed quite unable to meet.

Yet again there was that in Christianity which rose to the emergency. Proportionately the losses were less severe than they had been when the Roman Empire faded. The subsequent recovery and gains were less delayed, more impressive, and more extensive. Parted from its medieval integuments, Christianity was released to fresh achievements.

In Western Europe a revival more potent than Christianity had thus far displayed brought abounding life. In the North it was the Protestant Reformation. In the South it was the Catholic Reformation. In the North the masses were stirred by Christianity as they had never before been. In the Middle Ages most of the leaders of the religious movements had been from the landed aristocracy or, after the rise of the town, from the urban middle classes. For instance, Bernard of Clairvaux was of the aristocracy, and Francis of Assisi and Peter Waldo were from merchant stock. In the Roman Catholic revival the leadership was still largely from the aristocracy and was from south of the Alps where more of the tradition of the Roman Empire persisted. The Theatines, who, a limited group, embodied much of the new life, were chiefly recruited from members of that class. The much larger Society of Jesus had as its founder an aristocrat, Ignatius Loyola, and for its most flaming early spirit Francis Xavier, another from that social stratum. This aristocratic leadership may have accounted, at least in part, for the conservative nature of the Catholic Reformation. That movement sought to purge the inherited Church of its moral weaknesses and to quicken its spiritual life without substantially altering its organization, its creeds, or its ritual. On the other hand, the outstanding early figures in the Protestant Reformation, Luther and Zwingli, were from north of the Alps, where the Roman Empire had either not extended or had never taken firm rootage, and were of peasant stock. Calvin, from near the northern border of the Roman occupation, was also not very remote from peasant ancestry. The more radical wing of the Protestant Reformation had as formative figures many, like numbers of the Anabaptists and George Fox, who were drawn from the humble classes. In other words, the awakening of the sixteenth and seventeenth centuries followed the gripping of members of all classes by the Gospel. This was especially the case in what we call Protestantism.

We must note that Protestantism as the collective name of the movement to which it is affixed is a misnomer. Protestantism is not primarily a protest. It was in part that—a reaction against the more palpable abuses of the inherited church, abuses which many of those who remained within the Roman fold deplored and sought to eradicate. It was to a larger degree also a reformation, an attempt not only to free the Church from the moral corruption which the loyal Roman Catholics endeavored to eliminate but also to emancipate it from what the reformers deemed departure from true Christianity but which the Roman Catholics believed valid. Two of the cardinal doctrines of Protestantism, salvation by faith, at least as Protestants interpreted it, and its corollary, the priesthood of all believers, were rejected by Roman Catholics. In a sense the Protestant Reformation was the attempt to return to primitive Christianity. Yet while the movement was both a protest and a reform, it was much more. It was a fresh and vigorous upsurge from the Christian stream. It endeavored to return to the Christianity of the New Testament. Several of the more radical forms would reject, as deterioration, all the accretions of the succeeding centuries. Yet none perfectly reproduced the Christian communities of the first century. Some of the more extreme wing took belief in the Holy Spirit as inspiration for movements which could find no parallel in Christian history. Indeed, no phase of Protestantism, large or small, was entirely like anything that had gone before. The churches which were in the majority, such as the Lutheran, the Reformed, and the Anglican, strove, to a

greater or less extent and with varying degrees of success, to preserve continuity with the past. From the standpoint of historic
Christianity the churches which were the fruits of the Reformation were distinctly and decidedly Christian. Yet here was
a new movement. It was evidence of amazing vigor in the Gospel
that, after the collapse of the culture of Medieval Europe which
had been so closely associated with Christianity, this fresh tide
should flood forth. It was another example of what we have seen
earlier, that under some circumstances the disintegration of a
culture with which Christianity has been closely knit frees the
Gospel for new achievements.

This ability of Christianity to move forward with renewed
power after the disappearance of a culture with which it had
been closely connected was also seen in the effect of the faith
upon the civilization of the Europe which succeeded the Middle
Ages. Whether it was more or less would be difficult to establish,
for we here are dealing with factors which defy accurate measurement. However, the effects of Christianity upon the six-
teenth-, seventeenth-, and eighteenth-century Occident are in-
contestably great. They are in part a continuation of what was
seen in the Middle Ages. So far as they fall into this category
they might be ascribed as due to social lag, the habit of moribund institutions to persist after the period of their creative
heyday has passed. But here was much more than that. In
quite fresh ways and movements Christianity was powerful in
forming the new Occident.

This was seen in the political arena. Here Christianity made
for democracy. The first really pure democracies were the
churches of the extreme wing of Protestantism. This was to
have been expected. The central convictions of salvation by
faith and the priesthood of all believers make for the equality
of all Christians and hence for democracy. They likewise en-

courage by implication not only equality, but what is also essential to successful democracy, a sense of responsibility.

In the international realm, where new nation states under absolute monarchs were clashing in war, the Christian faith and conscience inspired the most hopeful early attempts to put the relations between governments on the basis of law. The great Spanish theologian, Francis of Vitoria, and the Dutch statesman and theologian, Hugo Grotius, both of them earnest Christians, were the leading pioneers in international law.

New types of education sprang out of the fresh religious movements. This was true of the schools of the Brethren of the Common Life and of the Jesuits and their *ratio studiorum*. It was also seen in some of the other new Roman Catholic orders and congregations and in the Port Royalists. Among the Protestants the Moravian Comenius was a prophet in his high regard for the child in education, the *volksschule* came out of early Lutheranism, and the *realschule* from the Pietist revival. The non-Conformist academies of England were the livest centers of higher education in the eighteenth century. In new movements to educate the masses earnest spirits among both Roman Catholics and Protestants took the initiative.

In literature Christianity was the inspiration of such works as *Paradise Lost* and in music it gave rise to such outstanding masters as Bach and Palestrina. Without it the new schools of painting and sculpture of the fifteenth, sixteenth, and seventeenth centuries would have been infinitely poorer. How far Sir Isaac Newton's deep religious faith was responsible for his contributions to science and mathematics we cannot know, but that some causal connection existed seems certain.

Christianity, too, showed sufficient vigor to follow and in some cases to precede the European explorers, merchants, and conquerors of the sixteenth, seventeenth, and eighteenth centuries. In some respects this was a phase of the expansion of Europe. Yet it was not an essential phase in the sense that it automatically followed that expansion. But for the life within Christianity it would not have occurred. It was chiefly from the Christian revivals of the sixteenth and seventeenth centuries, both Roman Catholic and Protestant. The new life which these embodied sent missionaries out by the hundreds and thousands. The overwhelming majority were Roman Catholics. Fewer were Protestants and still fewer were Russian Orthodox. This was chiefly because the leading exploring and colonizing powers of the sixteenth and seventeenth centuries were Spain and Portugal, staunchly Roman Catholic. The only Protestant powers which had much share in the expansion of Europe were England and the Netherlands, and these did not enter the scene in a large way until the seventeenth century. The Russians moved across a vast area, Siberia, but it was sparsely settled and presented no great challenge to the missionary.

The explorations, discoveries, and conquests commenced either before the religious revivals had begun or before they assumed major proportions. At their outset, therefore, not much effort was put forth to make them a means of spreading the faith and, in the Americas, the Indians were cruelly exploited. In Africa, moreover, the overseas slave trade was begun to supply the New World plantations.

As the religious awakening assumed major proportions it effected a striking change. Now the missionary often pressed ahead of the merchant and the conqueror. Sometimes the latter followed him. Sometimes he did not. In much of India, in most of China, and in Tibet the missionary penetrated where neither the merchant nor the official representative of a European government could go. In Spanish America the missionary went ahead of other white settlers, although often as the tool of the government. Moreover, the Christian conscience was stimulated to large-scale efforts to prevent the cruel exploitation of the aborigines. To protect the natives, humane legislation was put on the statute books, notably in the *Laws of the Indies* of Spain. This was written at the instance of earnest Christians who were outraged by what they had seen and heard. It was significant that the first Christian priest to be ordained in the New World was Las Casas and that it was he who more than any other toiled that the Indians might be given justice. Yet he was only one of many. The Jesuits in Paraguay succeeded for generations in keeping armed troops or recruiters of forced labor from the territories of their missions. In Portuguese areas, notably in Brazil, missionaries, especially Jesuits, stood out against the white settlers on behalf of the Indian. It was a Jesuit, Peter Claver, who did all that one heroic soul could do, single-handed, to better the lot of the Negro slaves at one of the major ports through which they were introduced to the New World. Moreover, it was through Christianity and the Church that almost all of such schools, colleges, and universities as existed in the European colonial possessions were founded and maintained.

By the middle of the eighteenth century Christianity was more widely spread geographically than it or any other faith had been and in its own inner life it had made notable advances since the close of the European Middle Ages. This was not only in spite but in part because of the passing of the medieval culture which Christianity had helped to create. Through what had once seemed to be spelling its doom Christianity had been liberated and it possessed so much inherent energy that it was able to move on to fresh victories.

We must note, however, that in the sixteenth, seventeenth,

and eighteenth centuries Christianity came to be associated more nearly exclusively with Western civilization than it had ever been. Except for the Russian Orthodox Church and a few Armenian merchant communities, the spread of Christianity was entirely from the churches of Western Europe. The outposts of Nestorian Christianity which had been so widely flung across Asia had all but vanished. There remained only encysted groups in Persia, Mesopotamia, and India. One form of Western civilization passed to give place to another and in each change Christianity survived and went on to enhanced victories, but the association with Western civilization, very close from the fourth century, became more intimate. The Christian communities which were so extensive by the beginning of the eighteenth century, even when they were of non-Occidental peoples, were almost all under European direction.

III

In the eighteenth century a series of revolutions began in Western culture which continued into the nineteenth and twentieth centuries and which partly swept away the existing order and brought in a new era. The French Revolution with its profound repercussions in Europe and the revolutions in the Americas which both preceded and succeeded it ushered in a new political order. Republics were set up which aspired to be democratic and more of popular representation in government was forced upon the remaining monarchs. The Age of Reason was a stage in the emergence of the Age of Science. Man's views and understanding of the physical universe increased with breathtaking speed. Man's knowledge of the stellar world, of the geological history of his own planet, of the various forms of life, and of the nature and composition of matter was almost completely made over. Concurrently with this expanding knowledge went its application to provide man with food, clothing, and shelter. The Industrial Revolution inaugurated the age of the machine. Wealth and population rapidly mounted. Cities mushroomed almost overnight. Vast shifts of people were seen, partly from rural areas and small towns to cities and partly from Europe to Siberia, the Americas, Australasia, and South Africa. The impact of Western European peoples and their culture on the rest of the world which had begun in the Crusades and had vastly expanded from the fifteenth to the eighteenth century was now accelerated and intensified. The interior of Africa was explored by the white man and most of the continent was divided among European powers. Nearly all of the islands of the Pacific and much of Asia were brought partially or completely under the sway of European governments. The commerce of the Occident penetrated to every inhabited country of the globe. The impact of the Occident began to work those revolutions in the cultures of non-European peoples to which we referred in the last chapter. That age was begun which in our own day has become so violent and so kaleidoscopic as to be almost another era.

Once more a period of marked transition threatened the very existence of a faith which had so succeeded in the age that was passing that it might seem to be identified with it. Could Christianity survive? Many freely predicted that it could not. Both among the intellectuals and the masses were those who believed that the now seemingly hoary religion was merely a fading relic of an outmoded stage of mankind's development. Thousands tacitly abandoned the faith by neglecting it or by rendering it only nominal lip service. A few openly repudiated it. Many Christians who wished to remain true were deeply troubled and wondered whether the Bible and the Gospel could be reconciled with the new knowledge.

Yet once again there was that in Christianity which arose to the challenge and impressed that faith more widely upon mankind than ever before.

As in earlier eras, great awakenings occurred in the churches. The three forms of Christianity which had displayed the most vigor in the preceding period continued to be the main channels of the faith, but in different proportions.

The Russian Orthodox Church was still the least robust, but it displayed some signs of fresh life.

The Roman Catholic Church gave evidence of striking inner vitality. It did this more and more through accustomed patterns. Here and there it developed new types of organization, such as the Society for the Propagation of the Faith, a widespread organization for the raising of funds for missions through the giving of the rank and file of the faithful. In general, however, the pulsing life which was unmistakably present followed conventional channels. Many new orders and congregations in the monastic tradition sprang into being. There were more of them than in any previous century. They were, too, increasingly for service in the world and not for purely cloistered piety—although there were also some of these. The Roman Catholic form of Christianity had never before gripped the complete devotion of so many thousands. Yet the Roman Catholic Church was more and more tending to be a self-conscious minority, more tightly knit than at any earlier time, active in spreading the faith, but also frankly unreconciled to some of the main currents of the age. No really new theological developments occurred. Attempts by "modernists" to effect some reconciliation with the new currents of thought were officially rejected and their exponents were either forced into acquiescence or were expelled from the church. The theological formulations by a great mind of the Middle Ages, Thomas Aquinas, were stressed as authoritative. No new ones of comparable stature appeared. The Papacy exercised more effective administrative control over the church than ever. Of this the formal enunciation of the doctrine of Papal infallibility was a symbol. The Popes, too, denounced some of the current dominant trends in Europe which seemed to them anti-Christian. In some respects the Roman Catholic Church had never been so vigorous. Yet more than at any time since Constantine made his peace with it, it was in opposition to the spirit of the age. It was less and less flexible and more confined to the patterns with which it was familiar in organization, thought, liturgy, and personal piety. For it the far outlook was, therefore, not promising.

Far otherwise was it with what we have become accustomed to call Protestantism—and under that term all the many phases of a multiform movement are meant, including that widespread fellowship which shows the impress of both the Protestant and Catholic traditions, the Anglican Communion. The main current of Christianity seemed more and more to be moving through it.

Within traditional Protestant countries that form of Christianity, as a conscious personal possession, was gripping the rank and file as never before. In a certain sense, Protestantism for the masses now for the first time became religious and not political or communal. Always, since the beginning of Protestantism, there had been individuals who from personal experience knew salvation by faith. However, they were in the minority, sometimes included in state churches, sometimes gathered in small "sects." For the majority in Protestant countries, Christianity was what it had been in Roman Catholic days, primarily a community affair, to which one outwardly conformed or for which one argued because it was enjoined by the reigning prince and supported by public opinion. The principle of *cuius regio eius religio* was actually much older than the Reformation and simply persisted as a means of determining the territorial boundaries of Protestantism and Roman Catholicism. The most cursory knowledge of the story of the conversion of Europe reveals the fact that the masses followed the princes to the baptismal font. This tradition of adherence to a religion being identical with membership in a particular political or social entity was much older than Christianity. It was generally characteristic of religion. Now, in the nineteenth century, widespread revivals touched millions who were historically Protestant and made salvation by faith not a community matter but a real and transforming personal experience.

These revivals were most marked among peoples who were expanding rapidly in wealth, power, and population. This was notably the case in Great Britain and the United States, overwhelmingly Protestant by heredity. To the revivals came contributions from the Continent of Europe, especially from Pietism and Moravianism. Pietism and the closely associated Moravianism had arisen partly out of the unspeakable sufferings of the Thirty Years' War. A small minority had been stirred to plumb the depths of the Christian faith and to learn more of its amazing power. What they had discovered contributed, especially by way of John Wesley, to the awakening in the Anglo-Saxon world.

As Spain and Portugal had led in the expansion of Europe in the fifteenth, sixteenth, and seventeenth centuries and with them as channels the Roman Catholic Church had then been outstanding in the spread of Christianity, so now the expansion of European peoples and culture was chiefly through Great Britain and secondly through the United States. Through them this vital and augmented Protestant Christianity spread proportionately more rapidly than did Roman Catholic Christianity. From being confined almost entirely to the British Isles and North-western Europe, Protestantism now became world-wide, with millions of adherents in the United States, in the British possessions of Canada, Australia, New Zealand, and South Africa, and in minority groups in most of the non-Occidental countries of the world.

Protestantism was more flexible and adaptable to fresh environments than was Roman Catholic Christianity. It developed more entirely new types of organizations, such as the Sunday schools, the Bible societies, and the Salvation Army. In this there was danger: the new might be so adaptable that it would minimize or surrender the Christian faith. In general, however, the flexibility in producing new methods and agencies to meet novel needs was an advantage and was witness to abounding vigor.

This Christianity, with strikingly revived power, spread more widely than it or any other religion had thus far done. As we have suggested, the expansion was by the Russian Orthodox, the Roman Catholic, and the Protestant forms of the faith, but was predominantly by the last two and proportionately much more by the third than by the second.

The spread was partly by migrations of peoples already Christian by heredity. This was chiefly in the United States, both on the westward-moving frontier and by immigration directly from the British Isles and Europe. Much of it was by immigration from the same regions to South America, Canada, Australasia, and South Africa. These millions did not remain Christian automatically. Many of them came from lands where the churches were supported by public taxation. They went to lands where for the most part the churches, to exist at all, must be supported by voluntary effort. To some degree by assistance from the British Isles, Europe, or the older portions of the United States, but chiefly through the activities of the settlers themselves, the bulk of the newly shifted populations remained Christian. Indeed, in the United States during the nineteenth century the percentage of the population having a church membership increased fairly steadily.

The spread of Christianity was also by winning converts among peoples where until then the faith had been represented either only by small minorities or not at all. The progress was rapid among the Negroes of the United States, the Indians of the United States and Canada, in the islands of the Pacific, among the Negroes of Africa, in India, in Burma, in China, in Korea, and in Japan.

In addition, strikingly successful efforts were made to reach the populations which had moved into the new industrial centers. This was especially notable in the first of the highly industrialized lands, Great Britain. Here the churches increased in vigor and membership and in their effective hold on the masses, and that in addition to the great efforts which were put forth to propagate the faith overseas. We need only recall, as examples, the many church edifices which were erected and such organizations as the Salvation Army and the Young Men's Christian Association.

Most of this expansion of the faith was accomplished by the voluntary offering of life and of money. In the Middle Ages the spread of Christianity had been partly through the leadership of princes. In the sixteenth, seventeenth, and eighteenth centuries it had been mainly financed and directed by governments or official commercial monopolies. More than at any previous time in history, not even excepting the first centuries, missions became the concern of the great body of Christians. This in itself was evidence of the growing vigor of the Christian constituency and of the fashion in which the Gospel was gripping the masses of Christians. To be sure, missions still were the interest of only a minority of those who bore the Christian name, but that minority was larger than it had ever been.

The Christianity which was thus spread was having a wide and deep effect upon the various cultures in which it was found. In the Occident it gave rise to many fresh movements for social reform. Among these were the antislavery impulse, scores of peace societies, the modern nursing profession (which, through Florence Nightingale, stemmed from Pastor Fliedener's deaconesses of Kaiserswerth), prison reform, temperance movements, and better care of the insane. It founded large systems of parochial schools and hundreds of colleges and universities. In non-Occidental lands it pioneered in new and better medical and nursing professions, in introducing needed systems of education, and in efforts to relieve and prevent famine. It reduced to writing more languages than had been given written form in all the previous history of mankind. It fought the exploitation of non-Occidental by Occidental peoples. It made for purer family life and improved the lot of women.

IV

By this history Christianity has shown as has no other religion the ability to survive the deaths of cultures and eras with which it had been closely associated. After each major collapse of such a culture Christianity for a time seemed to stagger and decline. Each time, however, it rallied and went on to enlarged spread and influence. At the close of the nineteenth century Christianity was more widely spread and, when mankind is viewed as a whole, more influential in the affairs of the human race than it or any other religion had ever been.

It will be noticed, moreover, that in each successive major

crisis the territorial losses of Christianity have been less marked, the period of decline and stagnation less prolonged, and the subsequent advance more striking than in the one before it.

It must also be mentioned that there is in what we call Western civilization a continuity in spite of crises and that since the majority of Western peoples made Christianity their professed faith there has been a series of stages, each creative. The civilizations of Egypt and Mesopotamia passed so completely that in neither region has there been for centuries marked creative activity. For at least nine centuries China has been progressively less creative. For nearly as long India has had little distinctively new. Not for about the same length of time have the southern and western shores of the Mediterranean seen much that is really novel, and that in spite of the fact that they, like the northern shores of that sea, were heirs of Greece and Rome, and even included Egypt and Babylonia. The triumph of Islam over Christianity is the striking difference. In Europe, and particularly among Western European peoples, in contrast, where Christianity has longest had free course, cultures have decayed, but each has been followed by a fresh stage which, while taking advantage of what survived from the past, has been marked by new and vigorous ideas and institutions.

This must not be confused with the doctrine of automatic progress, so popular in the optimistic nineteenth-century Occident. Nor does it mean that Western civilization, especially as we have known it, will go on to new achievements. It does seem to indicate, however, that thus far from Christianity has come a dynamic which has contributed not so much to recovery of what a transition has lost, although there is much of that, but to fresh achievements. Christianity does not prevent the death of cultures, but it not only survives some of the cultures where it has been the community faith, but also, where it is the religion of the community, from it come impulses which lead to new achievements.

This history is evidence that in the Gospel of which Christianity was the vehicle there is that which appeals to at least some men of every age and culture. It speaks to the persistent needs of men. This is because there is in the Gospel that which confirms the declaration of St. Augustine: "Thou hast made us for thyself and our heart can find no rest until it rests in thee."

Presumably a faith with such a record will continue, regardless of the shifting scene. Presumably, too, it will remain the salt and the light in whatever stage of civilization may succeed the present. That civilization will not fully conform to Christian ideals. There will be in it much which is quite antagonistic to the Gospel. Yet in so far as it is constructive it will be so because of the Gospel.

CHAPTER IV

RECENT LOSSES AND GAINS

THE promise given by the record of Christianity is being ful-filled in our stormy age. Again, as so often in Christianity's past, an old order is passing and a new is emerging. Christianity, by its very achievements connected with the culture which is passing, is threatened. As so often in its earlier days, moreover, the partial emancipation which is coming through the partial disappearance of the old order by which it had been bound, spells opportunity and challenge. As is to be expected, the present century has seen both losses and gains. The losses are spectacular. The gains are less obvious to the casual observer but are no less real. They seem only to have begun. They may well be harbingers of a great fresh age of advance.

I

The losses of the present era are for all to see. Several of them are continuations of what was under way in the nineteenth century. Others have come since 1914, the year which really marked the end of the age of the nineteenth century—as the close of the wars of Napoleon in 1815 marked its beginning.

Some of the losses which were noticeable in the nineteenth century have taken on larger proportions in the post-1914 world.

The shifts of population from rural regions to cities and from city to city have become more extensive and in spite of efforts the churches have not fully kept pace with them. Millions who had a church affiliation in their old environment have failed to establish one in the new. These shifts have been accelerated and augmented by the world wars of the twentieth century, especially by the second. The losses to Christianity from these moves have not usually been symptoms of hostility to the faith. They have largely arisen from indifference. To some degree they are phases of the disintegration of community life of which the Church is a part. Multitudes in our cities are deracinated individuals who have established almost no community ties of any kind, but live out their existences of work and amusement without assuming responsibility for the local community in which they find themselves.

Another continuing drift from Christianity is by intellectuals. This was a phenomenon of the Age of Reason and the Enlightenment of the eighteenth century. It was seen in the nineteenth century. Whether it is now more or less marked than it was in that century would be difficult to determine. In some university quarters in recent years a deep concern has arisen and something of a return to Christianity has been witnessed. Yet in the universities of much of the Continent of Europe the departure from Christianity is much more extensive than in the year 1914.

The inroads of nontheistic liberal humanism have continued to be marked, especially in the Americas. Here that humanism persists, somewhat belatedly, when it has been superseded in much of Europe by systems which are the opposite of liberal. Some of the nontheistic humanists, aware of the weaknesses of that view, have either fully accepted Christianity or are moving in that direction.

The losses due to secularism are unabated. More and more millions are absorbed in the search for the materially "good things" of life and for "security." That helps to account for the drift away from the churches in Great Britain which has been one of the startling phenomena of the post-1914 era. It also seems partly responsible for the loss by the overwhelming majority of the French of their historic Christianity.

Anti-Christian ideologies have combined with war and other factors to bring great distress to the churches of Europe. This was first and most strikingly seen in Russia, where after the triumph of Communism in 1917 the numbers affiliated with the churches rapidly dwindled. It was also seen in the large-scale defections in Nazi Germany.

Numerically, in proportion to the population Christianity is probably weaker today in its historic stronghold, Europe and the British Isles, than it has been since the first conversion of these lands.

Moreover, in some great areas in the non-Occident World War II brought grave difficulties and possibly numerical loss. Full figures are not available, but this seems to have been the situation in the East Indies, Burma, the Philippines, China, Japan, and Korea. Certainly in these countries serious pressure was put on the churches and there was marked destruction of physical property. In Korea, due to earlier Japanese pressure, and, in the North, because of Russian occupation, the churches have had a very rough time.

In all of this the losses of Christianity have been grave and must not be minimized. The threats which we summarized two chapters above have been and still are very real.

II

However, as so often in the past, so now, Christianity is displaying amazing vitality. In the period since 1914, when the forces which menace it have been so serious and so terrifying, and when the losses have been so severe, amazing gains have been achieved. Christianity is more widely spread geographically, more deeply rooted among more peoples, and more influential in the total life of mankind than ever before. Moreover, in an age when mankind, if it would escape self-destruction, must learn to co-operate on a global scale but when the nations have been pulling apart, Christians have been coming together and are beginning to build a world-wide fellowship which transcends national and even warring lines.

The processes by which this extension of Christianity is being accomplished are mainly a continuation of those which we saw in the last chapter. So far as the methods of Christian missions are concerned the year 1914 marked no sudden break. It was the world in which they operated for which that year introduced a new age.

In the present century, and especially since 1914, Christianity has become more widely disseminated and is more nearly evenly distributed geographically than it has ever been.

We have spoken of the numerical losses in Europe and Siberia and of the fact that even in Great Britain only a minority seem to have an affiliation with a church which leads to regularity of attendance. In the Near East there also appears to have been a numerical decline. This followed the massacres and forced migration of Armenians and Nestorians during World War I and the slow attrition of Islam upon the Coptic community in Egypt. In Japan World War II probably wrought a reduction in numbers. Reductions have been encountered in the revolutionary Moslem movement in Java. Almost everywhere else the record has been one of gain.

In the United States the percentage of the population who are members of churches has continued to rise until at the present it is over half. The percentage is larger in the older parts and smaller in the newer parts of the country. In general what is akin to a mass conversion has been in progress since the political independence of the nation. At the outset probably only about one in twenty had church membership. By 1910 the percentage was 43.4 and in the mid-1940's well over 50. In a certain sense these figures are deceptive. They may mean that church membership has become a social convention and that for the majority it has no other significance. We have no nation-wide figures to indicate what has happened in church attendance—to name a very crude criterion of loyalty—and certainly none to indicate how much ethical conduct has been affected.

For Latin America we have no statistics to enable us to estimate growth or loss. The contest in Mexico between church and state in the 1920's and 1930's seems to have weakened the Roman Catholic Church. Certainly several states forbade priests to say mass and numbers of church buildings were diverted to secular uses. In many other parts of Latin America the religious condition of the Roman Catholic population is very poor. This is freely acknowledged by some of the Roman Catholic clergy. However, the level, unsatisfactory though it is, seems to have risen slightly in the present century. This, as we are to see later, is due more to aid from Europe and the United States than to the church in Latin America itself. Protestantism in Latin America has made very substantial gains. This has been the case in all the republics, but it has been notable in Brazil and Mexico.

In the islands of the Pacific as a result of the missions of the nineteenth century several of the groups, principally on the western fringes, had in name become solidly Christian. They were largely Polynesians. Christianity was beginning to penetrate into the more numerous central and eastern groups of islands. Here it has made phenomenal progress since 1914. In the East Indies, too, Christianity spread rapidly between the two world wars. In that period of about a fifth of a century the Christian population more than doubled. We do not have comprehensive facts to know whether Japanese occupation and the subsequent political disorders have made for a decrease. In Java they seem to have done so, but the overwhelming majority of Christians are on the other islands, where the disturbances have not been so great. In the Philippines between the two world wars Protestantism spread by leaps and bounds and the Roman Catholic Church made great strides in improving its leadership.

In Negro Africa, Africa south of the Sahara, Christians have multiplied. In the three decades after 1914 the increase was more than fivefold—and that in a period when the population increased little if at all. The progressive disintegration of the native cultures of Africa has left a vacuum which presents Christianity with a challenge and an opportunity and into which it is moving. Scattered figures seem to indicate that, at least in some areas, the increase continued during World War II.

In the solid world of Islam Christianity has, if anything, lost ground numerically. But in some Moslem lands, notably Persia and Java, it has made slight gains. Whether they presage more extensive movements we cannot know.

India has witnessed a doubling of the totals of Christians between the years 1911 and 1941. Within those three decades they rose from about four millions to about eight millions. Since in that period the population of the country increased from 315,-156,000 to 388,197,000, the proportion of Christians advanced from about 1¼ per cent to a little over 2 per cent. Some of this growth was by an excess of births over deaths but the larger part was through conversions, mainly from the depressed classes. The mass movements into the Church from these hereditarily underprivileged groups have been one of the striking features of Indian life and present to the Church a problem as well as an opportunity.

In the smaller lands of the south and east of Asia the situation has varied from land to land. In Ceylon the growth in the Christian totals has not quite kept pace with that of the population as a whole, but the proportion is still about 10 per cent. In Burma, at least until the Japanese invasion in 1942, the percentage of Christians has mounted, but mainly by growth in one element in the population, the Karens. In Siam Christians, a very small minority, have increased but remain an inconsiderable percentage of the whole. In French Indo-China, where almost all the Christians are Roman Catholic, the totals rose by nearly a half in the twenty-one years between 1912 and 1933, or very much more rapidly than the population as a whole.

China has been disturbed during all the years since 1914. This has been partly through foreign wars and invasions but chiefly because of an internal revolution which for magnitude is greater than in any other nation, not even excepting Russia. The breakup of the old patterns of life has lessened the resistance to the spread of Christianity. On the other hand, the disorder due to civil strife and foreign war has retarded it, and secularism, intellectual skepticism, and anti-Christian Communism have proved grave obstacles. In spite of difficulties, so far as figures are obtainable, the proportion of Christians in China rose from $\frac{1}{2}$ per cent in 1914 to 1 per cent in about 1941. What the intensified wars of the 1940's have done to that total we do not know. We hear of increases in some districts and of decreases in others. In general Protestants appear to be more numerous than in 1937.

In Korea the totals of Christians mounted sharply but irregularly until the late 1930's. Then adverse political conditions wrought disorganization in the churches and the numbers of Christians have probably declined.

For Christianity in Japan conditions after 1914 were much of the time fairly favorable. This was until 1931. After 1931 the deterioration in Japan's relations with Western powers, especially the United States, from which came most of the missionaries, made for mounting difficulties. Down to the mid-1930's, however, the last dates when comprehensive figures are obtainable, the percentage of Christians in the population was rising. It was only about half of that in China and only about a fourth of that in India, but it was growing. War with the United States and the British Empire brought great restrictions on the churches and enemy bombings destroyed a large proportion of the church buildings. Church membership fell off. Yet a majority of the congregations maintained some kind of existence. Peace has brought renewed opportunity and hope to the Christian forces.

This rapid survey may seem somewhat statistical and therefore dull. It may also appear superficial. Many currents and countercurrents have been ignored and analyses have had to be by large population groups rather than by the many and diverse elements which are also essential parts of the picture. Yet enough has been given abundantly to substantiate the generalization that Christianity is more widely distributed than it was in 1914 and that it has made astonishing gains in the non-Occidental portions of the globe. The increase has been largely in connection with the missions of the churches of the Occident. Yet more and more in its membership Christianity is embracing all nations and races. In spite of threats, for the first time it has become world-wide. In this no other religion has ever equaled it or even approached it. It has also surpassed its own earlier achievements. None of the modern ideologies, not excepting Communism, is represented in so many different tribes, nations, islands, and countries.

Fully as significant as the numerical spread has been the fashion in which Christianity is putting down roots among many peoples and cultures. Here, too, it is going beyond its own former achievements and the records of other religions.

This is seen partly in the way in which Christianity is stimulating indigenous expressions of art. Sculptures and pictures of scenes and figures such as the Nativity and the Christ have increasingly appeared in African Negro, Indian, Chinese, and Japanese guise and by artists of these nationalities.

Probably more significant is the rapidity with which leadership has come forward in the non-Occidental churches. This is to be seen among both Roman Catholics and Protestants. It is partly because of the insistent nationalism which has mounted in the past three or four decades, with its restlessness under the white man's rule. Indigenous Christians have resented the taunts of their non-Christian neighbors that they are agents of white imperialism or are under the foreigners' control. They have wished to run their own churches. The Occidental leaders of the churches have heeded the demand. Often they have welcomed it and have long been preparing for it by the education of indigenous clergy and laity. However, no matter what the demand by the local Christians or the far-seeing statesmanship of Occidental churchmen, the development would not have attained its present proportions had Christianity not shown the vigor to grip men of ability and to stimulate them to assume burdens and to develop the requisite spiritual resources.

The trend toward indigenous leadership has been seen in the Roman Catholic Church. Great emphasis is being placed upon the training of native priests and transferring parishes to them. In 1933 nearly two-thirds of the Roman Catholics of Asia were under indigenous priests. Rapidly, too, indigenous priests are being raised to the episcopate. In 1926 six Chinese were consecrated bishops in St. Peter's in Rome by the Pope himself. Earlier there had been only one Chinese bishop, and he had been appointed in the seventeenth century. In 1939 on "Missions Sunday," again in Rome, the Pope consecrated twelve missionary bishops, symbolic of the apostleship of the Church to the entire world. They included an African from Uganda, a Malagasy from Madagascar, a Chinese, and an Indian. By the close of 1939 seven dioceses in India, three in Indo-China, one in Africa, two in Japan, and twenty-three in China were under indigenous bishops. Later all the bishops in Japan were Japanese. In the winter of 1945–46, in broadening the cardinalate, a Chinese was given the red hat. In 1946 China was given its own hierarchy of bishops and archbishops.

Protestants have also been developing indigenous leadership. They, too, have been placing members of the "younger churches," as they are called, in positions of responsibility. From the "younger churches" there have been appointed bishops, college and university presidents, executive officers of national bodies, and pastors of leading congregations. The development was dramatized in the gatherings to plan for the world-wide mission of the Church. In the World Missionary Conference held at Edinburgh in 1910 the overwhelming majority of the delegates were from the Occident. At its successor, convened in Jerusalem in 1928, about a quarter were from the "younger churches." At the next meeting in the series, held at Tambaram, near Madras, in December, 1938, less than half were from the Occident and more than half from the "younger churches." It was a matter of general comment at Tambaram that the strongest delegation was that of China and that its members were young—vivid evidence of the ability which was coming forward from non-Occidental churches.

Moreover, this Christianity of the non-Occident is beginning to make contributions to the Christianity of the Occident. T. Z.

Koo, a Chinese, as a secretary of the World's Student Christian Federation has traveled widely among student Christian movements in the Occident and has brought them deepened religious insight and broadened geographic horizons. Toyohiko Kagawa is almost as well known in Protestant church circles in the United States as in Japan and by his writings and public addresses has contributed markedly to the life of American Christianity. During World War II, when forces from the United States were stationed in the New Hebrides, one of the native pastors of that archipelago won several American service men to the Christian faith and at least one of the latter, as a result, is entering the Christian ministry.

In other words, Christianity, while still largely identified with the Occident, is becoming rooted outside the Occident and from that vantage point is contributing to the religious life of what was once called Christendom. The movement away from a purely or predominantly Occidental setting is gaining momentum. Here and there it has been slowed by the recent wars. The costs of the Japanese invasion in Chinese leadership have been tragic. Scores of outstanding laymen and pastors, carrying heavy burdens of relief or of protecting their flocks, have perished or have come through with greatly impaired health. Handicapped by war conditions, churches and schools have been unable fully to replenish their ranks. In Japan, Korea, the Philippines, the East Indies, and Burma, the toll of the war years has been heavy. Yet, in general, the trend is rapidly toward the broadening of the racial and cultural base of Christianity. However, even during war years and under the pressure of the emergency, in some churches in China financial self-support has mounted and lay leadership has assumed larger burdens. Christianity is still tied to the Occident. Were it to be overwhelmed there the effect elsewhere might be disastrous. Yet as never before in the history of the faith or of any other religion, Christianity is becoming rooted in every culture and among almost every people.

Viewed from the standpoint of mankind as a whole, the twentieth century is seeing a marked increase in the influence of Christianity. It would be hard to prove either that Christianity has grown or has declined in its effect upon the Occident. Numerically, as we have said, in Europe it has suffered severe losses. Yet among minorities the sufferings of these late years, and especially of World War II and its aftermath, have led to a deepening of Christian faith and to a fresh discovery of the eternal resources of the Gospel. We must recall, too, that the Christian faith has been of great importance in the creation of the League of Nations and of its successor, the United Nations. Many of the ideas incorporated in these two bodies were produced by peace societies of the nineteenth century which had Christian origins. The chief architect of the League of Nations, Woodrow Wilson, was inspired and sustained in his effort by a profound Christian faith. No one man had as large a part in shaping the Charter of the United Nations as did Wilson in bringing the League of Nations into existence, yet some features of the Charter are clearly traceable to Christian influence. Indeed, the churches as churches had a much greater share in preparing the way for the United Nations than they had in bringing the League of Nations into being.

Christianity has stimulated widespread efforts to relieve the suffering born of war. Notable have been Near East Relief in World War I, the Friends Service Committee, and the work of the Young Men's Christian Association for prisoners of war.

Continuing, too, have been hospitals and schools and other enterprises for the welfare of the community. These have so long been fruits of Christianity and their presence is so accepted as part of the life of the Occident that they are scarcely noticed. Yet they are there and in most countries of the Occident continue much as they did in the latter part of the nineteenth century. In Russia they have been superseded by the state. In Germany the schools had difficulties with the Fascist regime, and in Mexico the church schools have been regarded with suspicion. Yet in general the community activities inspired by Christianity have continued.

It has been outside the Occident that the influence of Christianity has increased the most notably in the present century. Very striking have been the contributions in China. The most influential Chinese of the present century, Sun Yat-sen, was largely shaped by Christianity. The son of a village farmer, "a coolie and the son of a coolie" as he called himself, he owed most of his formal education to Christian schools in Hawaii, Canton, and Hongkong. He was a baptized Christian and at one time considered entering the Christian ministry. He was, of course, not exclusively the product of Christianity. Many other elements entered into the formation of his character and ideals. Yet he confessed to the importance of the Christian contribution. Through him Christianity helped to shape the political, economic, and social ideals of the new China, for he has been accepted as standard by the Kuomintang, the most powerful party of the Republic, and he has also been honored by dissident groups. The Soong family, into which Sun married, and which has been potent in the government for a quarter of a century, has a strong Christian background and its present representatives have professed that faith. Chiang Kai-shek, as all the world knows, is a Christian, as are a number of other Chinese who are prominent in the life of the state. The Christian faith may not be dominant in the lives of any of these men and women, but it has been present and through them has exerted a far greater influence upon the government of China than it did in the nineteenth century. In education Christianity has had a larger share in China than it did before 1914. This is seen partly in the schools operated by the Christian forces. These have pioneered in medicine, nursing, agriculture, and forestry to a greater degree than they did before that year. The Mass Education Movement, for the purpose of teaching the illiterate masses to read and to reshape entire communities, has had as its leader a Christian, Dr. Yen, and was begun under the auspices of the Young Men's Christian Association.

The most influential figure in India in the present century, Gandhi, freely admits his indebtedness to the New Testament and to Christ. He makes no pretense of being a Christian. He is a Hindu. Yet in his use of peaceful nonviolence he has been in part inspired by Christ and in entering and terminating some of his fasts he has had Christian as well as Hindu hymns sung. Through him Christianity makes itself felt in Indian life far more than ever before. In other ways the impress of Christianity upon India has been deepening. One of the most extensive of these is the stimulus to the depressed classes in their efforts to improve their lot. In the present century the Christian Church has been their chief door of escape from agelong servitude and degradation. Hundreds of thousands have become Christians and through their new faith have entered into spiritual and moral emancipation and through Christian schools have found intellectual and economic improvement. Through their example hope, even though vaguely, has come to many of their non-Christian neighbors with demand for release from the inferior position which has been theirs. In India, too, the contribution of Christianity to bettering the condition of women has continued and enlarged.

China and India together comprise almost half the population of the globe. As seats of ancient civilizations they are also important. The growth of Christian influence upon them, even though that is still very much a minority influence, means a significant advance in the effect of Christianity upon mankind.

Upon another great mass of non-Occidental humanity, Negro Africa, the effect of Christianity has been rapidly mounting. This is seen in the striking growth in the number of Christians and in the morals, the family life, and the education of the Christians. Here and there, too, have been prophet movements for larger privileges for the Negroes which have had Christian impulses in their inception but which have displayed decidedly non-Christian features.

Japan has seen something of an increase in the influence of Christianity. That faith is far less potent in the islands than in the neighboring China. Yet it cannot be dismissed as negligible. In the lives of its members, in certain aspects of social reform, and in repercussions upon non-Christian religions it is more to be reckoned with than its numerical strength would appear to warrant.

In this attempt to estimate the influence of Christianity the most important aspect of all eludes precise measurement. It is that quality of living, that radical beginning of eternal life, that entrance here and now into the kingdom of God, which is of the essence of the "good news." It is that from which these other effects proceed. They are secondary. It is primary. We recognize it when we see it in individual lives, we are humbled and inspired by it, and we thank God for it. Yet it evades statistics.

However, although figures cannot contain it or measure it, we can be certain that in Christian living the Gospel is also more widely spread than ever before. The very geographic extent of Christianity is evidence. Somewhat more so is the fashion in which leadership is emerging from among non-Occidental Christians. More significant still is the quality of life and the insight into the meaning of the Gospel, not only among leaders who are known to the churches of the Occident, but also among many humble folk who are not so known.

There can be no doubt that within these past thirty years, when it has been threatened by gigantic and hostile forces, the Gospel has made itself felt more widely among mankind than ever before.

In one other respect, as we suggested at the outset of this chapter, the years since 1914 have witnessed a striking advance in Christianity. This is in the way in which Christians have been coming together. It is a process which thus far has only barely begun. It is far from complete. At times it seems to suffer reverses. It does not move as rapidly as many of us wish that it might. Yet, if we look back across the present century, the advance has been astounding and is evidence of amazing vitality.

The movement toward Christian unity is not new. It is as old as the Christian Church. From the first, Christians have been divided. From the beginning, too, they have been dreaming of a unity in which all Christians would love one another and thus demonstrate that they are disciples of one whose great command was love and whose "new commandment" was that his followers should love one another.

Yet much of the movement toward Christian unity has not been from the New Testament motive of expressing that love. It has, rather, been for the purpose of safeguarding what Christians have believed to be the revelation of God's truth and thus to assure the salvation of souls. This purpose, laudable and understandable though it is, has led to bitter debates and to divisions. The eternal welfare of men and women has been judged to be at stake and Christians have stood tenaciously for the formulation of the faith and the means of grace by which they have been convinced that this could be accomplished.

Under the inclusive political and social structure of the Roman Empire what looked like unity was achieved in the Catholic Church. That church in the third century embraced a larger proportion of those who professed and called themselves Christians than have before or since been brought within one inclusive organization. Earlier the "Judaizers," then the Gnostics, the Marcionites, and the Novatians, kept great portions of those who thought of themselves as Christians from fellowship in this "Catholic" Church. Later the Arians, then the Nestorians, the Monophysites, and others were to be apart from it.

As the centuries passed, the eastern and western wings of the Catholic Church drifted apart into the Orthodox Churches and the Roman Catholic Church. This was due largely to the breakup of that state, the Roman Empire, in association with which the Catholic Church had come into being. During the later Middle Ages thousands, many of them humble souls who sought only to follow Christ, were forced outside the Roman Catholic Church. Then came the Protestant movement and the expulsion of most of the Christians of Northwestern Europe from the Roman Catholic Church.

It must be clear to all whose loyalty has not distorted their judgment, that the road to Christian unity does not lie through the Roman Catholic Church. Although it is more widespread geographically than ever before and has in it much vigor, that great church progressively includes smaller and smaller proportions of those who regard themselves as Christians. This assertion, startling though it may seem, is supported by the facts of history and, did space allow, could here be demonstrated. The Roman Catholic Church is increasingly too inflexible, too bound by the traditions of a past environment, to be the way to Christian unity. Thousands of its devout members pray for Christian unity and hope that their prayers will be answered by the "return home," as they phrase it, of other Christians. God must honor the passion for unity and the desire for the eternal salvation of souls which lie back of those prayers. But, as so often, His ways are not our ways, and, while He will not permit His word to return to Him void, He seems to be answering their prayers in ways far different from those which they had anticipated, and, after His own way, in a far richer fashion than they had dreamed possible.

The present movement toward Christian unity is, as we all know, coming through Protestantism. No more than the Roman Catholic road is it the final way. The prayers of those who look to it as the solution of the agelong yearning of devout Christians will not be answered fully in the manner which they now anticipate. Yet here is a movement which already has brought together a larger variety of Christians than has any other in history. It is given by its supporters the designation Ecumenical. By that is meant that it is as broad as the inhabited world. Geographically it has not yet attained that dimension. Yet it is making amazing strides and has in it more hope as a road toward a unity which ultimately will draw into it, in one fashion or another, all who "profess and call themselves Christians."

This is not the place to sketch the history or even fully to describe the Ecumenical Movement. That would take an entire and much longer book. Here we can merely briefly name some of the outstanding characteristics of the Ecumenical Movement and point out that here is part of the evidence that in this day of transition and testing Christianity is displaying an amazing life. Once again, as in other eras when old cultures have passed, the very throes of the age are evoking the power inherent in the

Gospel. The death agonies of the old world which it knew are impelling Christianity to fresh achievements.

First of all, it must be noted that the Ecumenical Movement stems primarily from what in its most comprehensive aspects is that which we have called Protestantism—and in that we are including the Anglican Communion.

This is both surprising and natural. It is surprising because Protestantism is, in its essence, the most fissiparous form of Christianity. Its primary distinctive doctrines, salvation by faith and the priesthood of all believers, lead to endless division. A cynical Roman Catholic writer called it, in describing it in China, "from Confucius to confusion." New movements which some denominate "sects" are from time to time emerging from it. Indeed, they are often a sign of life. It is through this apparently endlessly dividing Protestantism that the present trend toward Christian unity is coming.

Yet this is to be expected of Protestantism. It arises partly from the fact that, being so divided, Protestantism is more flexible and therefore more responsive to the inner spirit of the Gospel and to the demands of the age than are the more stereotyped forms of Christianity. The others are progressively less flexible and more ossified.

The Ecumenical Movement springs partly, too, from the desire of the most earnest Protestants to realize fully the Gospel and to make it known to the world. Thus the Gospel, less hampered by the accretions from the past environments than in other major forms of Christianity, is better able to find expression. In expressing itself it seeks to draw all Christians together in love.

Next, we must call attention to the fact that the Ecumenical Movement has arisen, not from a desire to make Christian unity an end in itself, but as a means to an end. That end is obedience to the Great Commission to make disciples of all nations, baptizing them in the name of the Father and of the Son and of the Holy Spirit, teaching them to observe all that our Lord commanded his immediate disciples. As we are to see more at length later, we have only begun to comprehend the scope of that command. It has as its impossible goal leading all the human race into conformity to the standards of the Sermon on the Mount, standards so high that those of little faith have thought of them as ad interim ethics, meant to be followed only by the little flock in the brief interval between their enunciation and the final, apocalyptic judgment. In this respect the Ecumenical Movement has springs similar to those of the earlier Catholic Church of the Roman Empire. It has, however, followed a somewhat different road. The earliest foreshadowings of the present Ecumenical Movement arose from the dream of pioneers who wished to share the Gospel with the entire world. It was William Carey who, in the midst of another period of world upheaval, the French Revolution and the Napoleonic Wars, called for decennial conferences of all Protestantism to plan on a global scale for the fulfillment of the Great Commission. The Ecumenical Movement is a present-day endeavor to bring together all Christians to make effective the Great Commission in all aspects of life.

A striking example of the Ecumenical Movement has been the Orphaned Missions Fund formed by the International Missionary Council during World War II and maintained during the aftermath of that war. It has had as its purpose the support of those Protestant missions which were cut off by the war from their European constituencies. Financial aid was given regardless of nationality or denomination. Funds from Christians in the United Nations went to the rescue of German missions and to Lutheran missions not only from Lutherans but also from Presbyterians, Baptists, Congregationalists, and Methodists. Here was something new in Christian history.

In the third place, we must notice that the Ecumenical Movement is expressing itself in a wide variety of organizations. It is not identical with any of them. One of the earliest, now not so prominent as formerly, is the World's Evangelical Alliance. Through their constituent bodies the world committees of the Young Men's Christian Associations and the Young Women's Christian Associations bring together Christians of many communions, including some from the Orthodox churches and the Roman Catholic Church. The World's Sunday School Association embraces men and women from many denominations. The World's Student Christian Federation, formed in 1895, draws together men and women in their student days and gives them a vision of the Church which is more inclusive than any of the historic communions. Out of it have come many of the leaders of other phases of the Ecumenical Movement. The International Missionary Council is in some respects the most inclusive of the ecumenical bodies. Although it was not formally constituted until after World War I, its rootage goes back well into the nineteenth century and it is the outgrowth of a long development. The World Conference on Faith and Order and the Universal Christian Council for Life and Work are being merged in the World Council of Churches. That fellowship, although still in process of formation, is functioning actively.

There are, in addition, many local, state, provincial, and national organizations for co-operation across denominational lines. These include many state federations of churches, several National Christian Councils, the Federal Council of the Churches of Christ in America, and the British Council of Churches.

Here and there are fusions of separate communions, such as

the United Church of Canada and the Church of Christ in China. More numerous are the unions of closely related bodies, such as those of the English Methodists and the American Methodists.

All of these bodies are predominantly Protestant, but several draw in non-Protestants. That, as we have suggested, is true of the Young Men's and the Young Women's Christian Associations. It is also true of the World's Student Christian Federation. In the Missionary Conferences of Northern and Southern Rhodesia both Roman Catholics and Protestants have co-operated. The Federal Council of the Churches of Christ in America and the World Council of Churches include some non-Protestant churches. In the National Conference of Christians and Jews, formed in the United States at the instance of Protestants after World War I to promote better understanding, Protestants, Roman Catholics, and Jews are actively associated. The historic gulfs have not been eliminated. They have not even all been bridged. Especially do those between Protestants and Roman Catholics, and between the Orthodox and other Eastern churches and the churches of the West remain. There is no sign of their early or even eventual elimination. Yet, slight though it is, there is more co-operation between members of these major divisions of organized Christianity than ever before. This has been seen in Germany between Roman Catholics and Protestants under the stress of war. In spite of enhanced strain in the United States between the two wings of the Church, fellowship is growing, largely in quiet, unobtrusive ways, between clergy as well as laity on both sides of the division.

In the next place, it must be said that the Ecumenical Movement is not due to theological indifference. It arises from no easygoing tolerance among those for whom Christian beliefs count but little. It is primarily among the leaders of the churches, both clerical and lay, men and women who are most committed to their respective communions, but who feel the urgency of the tasks which must be faced together and who are so moved by the shame and inefficiency of the quarrels and suspicions among Christians that they seek to overpass them.

We must also point out that the Ecumenical Movement is not a spasm of fear and reaction from the international tensions and wars of our day. It began in the comparatively peaceful years of the century between 1815 and 1914. Since then it has gained in momentum. The growth has been rendered more difficult by the wars of the age. It has also, because of the vitality inherent in Christianity, been stimulated by them. The Ecumenical Movement was actually strengthened during World War II and across warring lines.

Lastly, we must say that the Ecumenical Movement seems to be only in its infancy and that no one can forecast with assurance its future direction or its culmination. To that we will later return.

In these four ways, then, in the face of its enemies, Christianity is again displaying amazing vitality. More than ever before it is spreading geographically, it is becoming more deeply rooted among a great variety of peoples, it is exerting influence upon mankind as a whole, and its adherents of many traditions are beginning to work together and in that work find common fellowship. Christianity, as it has been from the beginning, is a minority movement. In our day the world about it is more hostile than it has been for centuries. Some losses have been suffered. Yet, when it is viewed against the entire world, Christianity is more to be reckoned with than ever before. Unlike the other religions which rise, spread, become stagnant, and decay, Christianity comes through each major crisis with enhanced strength. Its appeal is to the universal and timeless in man. Because it is the power of God unto salvation it continues, always dying and behold it lives.

CHAPTER V

TRENDS IN THE SETTING

CHRISTIANITY is going on. It may lose ground in large areas as it has in the past, but, also as in the past, it will survive and from each crisis emerge with renewed and enhanced influence. That is its record. That record is being repeated in our age. The degree of free will which God has given man will modify the course of the faith and its temporal expressions, but ultimately God will not be defeated. His Gospel will accomplish His purposes for it.

But what kinds of Christianity will go on? What forms of the faith will dwindle? What forms will grow? From what branch or branches of Christianity may we expect the next great advances to be made? Can we forecast the modifications which the near or the far future will see in Christianity? Along what channel or channels are the main movements to be? What guises is the Christianity of the future to have?

Obviously the answer to these questions will be determined partly by the environment and partly by the vigor inherent in one or another of the various kinds of Christianity.

In our present chapter we must view the setting. We must ask what the environment is region by region and in some instances country by country and social group by social group, what changes in each are affecting Christianity, and what the effects are upon the several kinds of Christianity. From this we can glean some indication of what the future holds in store. We must again remind ourselves that prophecy is notoriously fallible. New factors may enter and completely alter the scene in quite unpredictable ways. Who, for instance, fifty years ago could have pictured the Russia or the Germany of today? Who then could have foreseen the American occupation of Japan, the republic in China, or the conflict between the Kuomintang and the Communists in that unhappy land? As we now look back over the half century we can see the processes by which the unexpected happened, but no one could have forecast it. On the other hand, some main trends could then have been foreseen and actually were predicted. Among them, as we earlier said, is the present prominence of the United States and Russia. The disappearance of the Manchus and internal weakness and disorder in China were reasonably assured. The ambitions of the ruling militarists in Japan were beginning to be apparent. The study of trends has its place and, if circumspectly made, can be the basis for daring and effective action.

I

First of the significant trends is the waning of Western Europe in the world scene. For the past four and a half centuries the Western end of the Continent of Eurasia has been aggressive and its peoples have progressively dominated the world. From the long standpoint of history, four and a half centuries are only a little more than a moment, "a watch in the night." Probably that hegemony could not endure. The machines and the science by which it was achieved would ultimately spread to other peoples. The nations, great and small, which have arisen from the migrations of European peoples in the Americas and Australasia would contest the supremacy of the mother countries. Non-Occidental peoples, recovering from the shock of economic and political conquest and adopting the appliances of the unwelcome masters, would throw off the white man's yoke. The myth of white racial superiority would be exploded.

That process has been hastened by war. The decline of Western Europe has been speeded up by the world wars of the present century. The first of these centered in Western Europe and there wrought its chief damage. The second, coming only twenty-one years after the first, added incalculably to the destruction. Partial recovery will, we hope, be achieved. It will, however, be only partial. Western Europe, impoverished, will not regain its former prosperity. Over it hangs a threat of insecurity greater than it has known for centuries. Pessimism and despair are the order of the day. The schools, laboratories, and universities cannot expect to regain the proud position which was theirs only a short generation ago. First-class minds there certainly still are. The tragedies of the age have stirred some of them to profound thought. However, the golden age of Europe appears to have passed. Moreover, the decay of Europe has coincided with violent attacks on Christianity, and, as we have noted, with marked defections from it.

What does this mean for Christianity? Western Europe has been the center of the Roman Catholic Church and the earliest home of Protestantism. Here the Roman Catholic Church has its administrative seat. Here has developed much of its greatest theology. Here have arisen all but a few of its monastic orders. From here have come most of its missionaries and the funds to support them. Here have flourished the majority of its saints. Here has been written the larger part of its devotional literature. The permanent impoverishment of Western Europe cannot but be a severe blow to the Roman Catholic Church. It will not prove fatal. Once before, in the collapse of the Roman Empire in the West, the Roman Catholic Church faced fully as great a disaster. It rallied and went on to fresh triumphs. Some of its choicest spirits, among them Pope Gregory the Great and Benedict of Nursia, were from the Italy which had suffered horribly from decay and invasion. It may well be that the vitality inherent in that Church will again stimulate some from Western Europe to greatness in character and achievement. Yet the waning of Western Europe cannot fail to be serious for the Roman Catholic Church. It has probably only begun and its full denouement will not be seen for a generation, perhaps for generations. Europe certainly cannot supply the Roman Catholic Church with the physical basis for its maintenance or its missions on the scale of the nineteenth century. Probably it cannot provide in such numbers as formerly the missionaries who have led in spreading the faith among non-Occidental peoples.

For Protestantism the blow is not as ominous. Not so much of that branch of Christianity is concentrated in Western Europe. Its chief numerical strength is in the British Isles, North America, and Australasia. So far as it has centers of administration, these are in London and New York rather than in Berlin or Amsterdam. The fact that the World Council of Churches has its headquarters in Geneva is an exception, but an exception to a general trend. Most of the Protestant missionaries and of the funds for their support have not been derived from Europe.

Yet the decay of Western Europe will weaken some aspects of Protestantism. It will be especially hard on the Lutheran and Reformed strains. Here has been their traditional home. Here has centered much of their scholarship, particularly that of Lutheranism. Here have developed most of their outstanding theologies. The weakening of the Lutheran and Reformed churches cannot but affect the rest of Protestantism. Just what those effects may be we will inquire in a later chapter.

We must note, however, that among the Protestants as among the Roman Catholics of Western Europe the sufferings of the age may stimulate new awakenings. Out of the desolations of the Thirty Years' War, from the very churches and sections in which those were the most severe, minorities emerged who had been driven by the tragedies of the day to fresh discoveries of the depth and the power of the eternal Gospel. So it may be now. The whole Church may be enriched by the Christian minorities in Europe—by the Confessional Church in Germany, by the underground resisters in Holland, Norway, and France, by the Christian pacifists who suffered imprisonment, and by the Christians who have survived the internment camps.

II

What of the British Isles? Obviously they remain one of the major powers. Obviously, too, if regarded apart from the Empire and the Dominions, as they must be from the standpoint of the future of Christianity, they do not loom as prominently as they did in the nineteenth century. They have not suffered as severely as has Western Europe, but the world wars of the twentieth century have taken heavy toll.

Moreover, as in the case of Western Europe, these wars have simply accelerated and accentuated a process which was already under way. Britain's outstanding position in the nineteenth century was due to conditions which could not endure. It was partly from the victory over Napoleon and the mastery of the seas. It was also, and more especially, because Great Britain led in the Industrial Revolution. It was this which helped to assure her defeat of Napoleon and to give her control of the oceans. For much of the nineteenth century she had a near-monopoly on the new machines which helped to make the age distinctive. She imported raw materials, turned them into manufactured goods, and sold them throughout the world. She was the world's chief manufacturing center. That monopoly could not be maintained. Other peoples either acquired machines from Britain or invented and made their own. All this does not necessarily mean the impoverishment of Britain. If commerce were reasonably free from artificial restrictions Britain could exchange the products in which she excels for those of other manufacturing countries as well as for raw materials. But man-erected barriers hamper trade.

As a result of World War II the British Isles have lost through enemy action much of the shipping on which they depended for part of their livelihood and to obtain the means of fighting cashed in a large proportion of the overseas investments returns from which aided their standard of living. India, too, seems about to move out of the British Empire and should she secede the loss of prestige and of aid in possible future wars will be serious. A large proportion of the physical equipment of the British Isles was destroyed by the bombings of World War II and its replacement places an additional burden upon an already heavily strained economy.

The British Isles are clearly not as rich as formerly. They are not likely fully to regain their wealth. They are confronted by a falling birth rate, by a stationary and eventually a declining population, and by the exodus to other lands of some of the more ambitious of their sons. This means an aging population with a decreasing proportion of the groups from which come energy and initiative. It is estimated that by 1970 the totals of men from fifteen to forty-four years of age will have fallen from 7.6 millions (in 1940) to 5.7 millions.

The British Isles are no longer as secure from foreign invasion as they were in the fore part of the present century. The English Channel has become a narrow ditch.

The decline in the relative position of the British Isles cannot but affect the outlook for Christianity. During most of the nineteenth century the United Kingdom provided the majority of the Protestant missionaries and the means for their support. From her came most of the creative thinking of that enterprise. By the close of the nineteenth century that hegemony was beginning to pass to the United States. The emergence in the latter country in the 1880's of the Student Volunteer Movement for Foreign Missions and the spread of that movement to the British Isles and to other lands were at once a symbol and a cause of the mounting share of the great American republic in the Protestant world mission. Yet the events of the present century have accelerated the shift.

In Britain itself the present century and especially the last few years have seen a decrease in the numerical strength of the churches. In the nineteenth century the rise in prosperity and population was paralleled by a striking increase in the vigor and strength of the churches. In England and Scotland the state churches experienced marked awakenings. In England and Wales several of the Non-Conformist bodies grew amazingly in numbers and in vitality. The churches of the British Isles are vigorous. They possess mature and skilled leadership. From their youth ability and devotion continue to come to take the place of the elders as the latter pass off the scene. Yet the majority of the population, especially of the oncoming generation, are comparatively untouched by the Gospel and are religiously illiterate. The slogan "the evangelization of England" witnesses both to the need and to the vision and faith of the Christian forces.

The relative decline of Britain makes for a shift in the proportions of the various kinds of Christianity in the world scene. Probably it does not weaken the aggregate strength of Protestantism. It may be expected to mean, however, the diminution of the British strains of Protestantism in the total global picture.

Presbyterians, Methodists, Baptists, and Congregationalists will be somewhat affected, although the strength of these communions in the United States and of the first two in the Dominions is so great that they will not be seriously disturbed. The distinctively British contributions in temper, thought, and quality of religious life in the world-wide Presbyterian, Methodist, Baptist, and Congregational fellowships will, however, decrease. The Anglican Communion will be more seriously affected. Its historic center is the Church of England. In England lies its greatest strength in tradition, leadership, and, probably, in numbers. In the United States it is a small minority. It looms much larger in Canada, Australia, New Zealand, and South Africa, but the total white populations of these countries do not exceed those of the two largest of the states of the American union. Through missions the Anglican Communion has been planted widely in Africa and Asia, but these missions are predominantly from England. If the Church of England wanes some of the churches nourished by these missions will go on, but others will decline and all will suffer.

III

The main power of Occidental civilization has moved away from Western Europe and has shifted to what was once the periphery, to Russia, the Americas, and the British Dominions. Power is now chiefly in Russia and the United States. In point of wealth and physical strength these are the two great states of our day and are to remain so for at least another generation and probably for much longer.

Russia is less representative of the historic Occident than is the United States, but in culture it stems more from the Graeco-Roman-Christian source than from any other, or, indeed, than from all others combined. Russia controls most of Europe. It is dominant in the eastern and central parts of the Continent. Only the western and southern fringes from Scandinavia south through Italy, and, across the Adriatic, Greece, are not under it. These, highly civilized and, with Great Britain, the traditional center of Western civilization, are profoundly affected by the Soviet colossus and in some of the states there are Communist parties or elements which look to Moscow for direction. In many other lands Communist groups exist, some of them strong, which can be counted on to take their cue from Russia. They may not be directly under Russian dictation, but they are sympathetic with Russia and Russia with them.

In general the Russian influence is hostile to Christianity. The official position of Russian Communism has been expressed in the familiar phrase: "religion is the opiate of the people." Since Christianity is the strongest of the religions and under the Czars was dominant in Russia, against it has been chiefly directed the antireligious animus of Communism.

For the moment the Soviet regime is less hostile than formerly to most of the Christianity within its borders. The militant League of the Godless which had its sympathy has largely disappeared. The Russian Orthodox Church has been allowed to elect a patriarch and to resume more of its life than was long permitted. The Evangelical groups and the Old Believers have not been stamped out. This, however, seems to indicate no basic change in the attitude of the Soviets and the all-powerful Communist party. The Soviet government has become strongly nationalistic. It is intensely Russian and will do what it believes strengthens Russia. The Russian Orthodox Church has proved useful. It has been associated with Russia's cultural past. It aided morale in the expulsion of the Germans. It has strong sister churches in Central Europe and the Balkans and can be helpful in promoting Russian influence in these regions.

Yet this attitude can be deceptive and can be fully as danger-ous as more open hostility. Russian Communism is basically no less antireligious than it was in the heyday of the revolution. It has found the Orthodox Church convenient and has sought to utilize it. This can be more destructive than persecution of that Church's witness to the Gospel. No church can ever be the tool of any government or any other ideology without compro-mising the Gospel and prostituting its mission.

Morover, between Soviet Russia and the Roman Catholic Church a deep-seated and irreconcilable hostility exists. The Vatican and the Kremlin are open enemies. This means added danger for the Roman Catholic wing of Christianity, already menaced through the weakening of its traditional stronghold, Southwestern Europe. Russian control in Poland, Hungary, and Austria and Russian influence in Czechoslovakia are a threat to the Roman Catholic Church in these lands—in all of which it has been religiously dominant. The situation in Poland is peculiarly acute and the "return" of the Ruthenian Uniates to the Orthodox fold is only one of many indications of the direc-tion in which the tide is running. The Roman Catholic Church, clinging to the southwestern fringes of Europe and suffering from long-term secularist defections in that area, does well to be alarmed. Even in one of its traditional strongholds, Spain, the Roman Catholic Church has been disturbed by Communism and driven into an uneasy alliance with Franco and the Falange.

The Russian threat to Protestantism is not so serious. To be sure, Lutheranism has suffered in the former Baltic states of Latvia and Esthonia and in the portions of Silesia from which the Germans have been expelled. Some have declared that in the latter region Protestantism has experienced its most serious territorial losses since the Thirty Years' War and the Revocation of the Edict of Nantes. Russia is an obstacle to Protestantism in

Hungary, Transylvania, the Russian zone of Germany, and Finland. Yet these areas do not constitute such important strongholds for Protestantism as does Europe for the Roman Catholic Church. The main bulwarks of Protestantism are elsewhere. In Russia, as we have suggested, the Evangelicals seem to be flourishing—or at least to be free from major persecutions.

In some lands where Christians are in the minority Communism and Russian influence or control are a menace. This is the case in the Russian zone in Korea, where, so far as can be learned, the churches are suffering. Christianity is encountering difficulties in the Communist parts of China—although here the direct aid of Moscow appears to be negligible.

Russia is a distinct threat to Christianity. However, its influence is strongest in areas of traditional Christendom in which that faith was least vigorous—in Eastern and Central Europe. It has not yet dealt serious open blows to the Roman Catholic Church in the latter's main stronghold, Southwestern Europe. It has affected only minorities of Protestants.

IV

The increasing place of the United States in the world has important repercussions upon the outlook for Christianity. These are to be found partly in the shifting strength between and within the major wings of Christianity.

The Eastern churches, including the Orthodox, are very small minorities. Most of them are represented, but none of them has the numerical strength or sufficiently outstanding spiritual vitality to affect notably the course of world-wide Christianity or of the other members of their own communions.

With the Roman Catholics the case is somewhat otherwise. They are a minority of the population, but a substantial and well-organized minority. They constitute the largest vigorous block of their communion outside of Europe. The Roman Catholics of Canada are fully as vital, but they are not as numerous. The nominal Roman Catholics of Latin America are more numerous, but their morale is very much lower and they are less well led. Not in all Asia and Africa combined do Roman Catholics attain the total of their brethren in the United States.

Moreover, the Roman Catholic Church in the United States is growing rapidly in wealth. At the outset its members were largely poverty stricken. They came from the other side of the Atlantic to better their financial lot. Hundreds of thousands of those who arrived in the first half of the nineteenth century were refugees from the Irish famine and landed with little more than the rags which they had on their backs. Most of those of other nationalities were from the less prosperous peasant stock or from the village and urban proletariat. Until after 1914 the Roman Catholic Church had its energies absorbed in gathering its hereditary children into parishes, in erecting churches and schools, and in recruiting and training members of the religious orders and clergy. After 1914 it caught up with its task. Because of World War I and then because of more stringent immigration laws, the flood from Europe dwindled to a trickle. The longer the Roman Catholic population is in the country the more it shares in the general wealth of the land. A very large proportion of those whose ancestors have been of that faith remain loyal.

Increasingly the Roman Catholics in the United States are the source of the financial sinews of their church. More and more they are taking a share—although still a minority share—in the world-wide missionary enterprise. It remains to be seen whether the resources of the United States in money and personnel can make good the losses in Europe. Thus far they have not. But the contributions are increasing.

The proportionate weight of the Roman Catholics of the

United States within their church as a whole is mounting. Presumably it will continue to do so. As the wealth and personnel of that wing of the church grow and as those of the European wing decline, the United States will count for more and more in the church.

This means that the temper of the Roman Catholic Church in the United States will increasingly mold that of the entire church. This will bring no change in dogma and probably little in ritual. Thus far no fundamentally new kinds of orders or major organizations have arisen in the United States, nor any fresh form of mysticism, devotion, or charitable undertaking. Yet there is a difference in temper. The church in the United States is more activistic than is that in Europe. For at least some time to come it will add no creative thought in theology. This is partly because from the necessity of making a place for itself in the new land it has heretofore had to live in the brick and mortar stage. It is partly because the general atmosphere of the United States is that of doing, of action.

Then, too, the quality of the clergy and the episcopate is not such as to offer much promise of distinction. The leadership of the church in the United States has been largely Irish. This is understandable. The Irish constituted the major element in the early Roman Catholic immigration, with the Germans a close second. Since in Ireland the Roman Catholic Church had for them been the one institution which they could call their own, it was the symbol and expression of their racialism and nationalism. The Irish, therefore, were passionately attached to it. In the United States they have displayed a capacity for a kind of political skill. Witness their control of the governments of some of the cities in the Northeast. They have carried this over into the church. Yet the Irish-Americans of Roman Catholic stock have thus far not produced a statesman of first or even second water. Presumably they will not do so in the church. From them will come bishops who will be able ecclesiastical manipulators. Here and there, as in the case of the late Bishop Walsh, co-founder and first head of the Catholic Foreign Mission Society, there will be men of wide-ranging vision, but the record scarcely leads us to expect either churchmen, scholars, or saints comparable in stature with some of earlier centuries and of Europe. Nor has the German stock thus far made a better showing. The Italians, although very prominent, are, for the most part, luke-warm toward the church and cannot be counted on for outstanding leaders. This is the more so because a large percentage are from the unpromising material from the south of Italy. Nor does there seem to be much hope from the other national elements in the church. To judge from its present membership and past record, the Roman Catholic Church can expect from its adherents in the United States money, a considerable amount of zeal, competence in organization, but rarely a high degree of creative intelligence, daring and wise statesmanship, or outstanding saintliness.

The United States is becoming the chief center of Protestantism, both numerically and in wealth. It is very much more Protestant than Roman Catholic. The United States is increasingly prominent in Protestantism. This is partly because of the increase of the population of the country. It is also because, in the growth of the percentage of the population who are church members, a growth which we noted in the last chapter, the proportionate increase of Protestants has been greater than that of Roman Catholics. Then, too, the weakening of Protestantism in Western Europe and the British Isles contributes to the enlarging place of American Protestants in that wing of organized Christianity. This is true not only of the losses of Protestantism in Europe in numbers, in clerical personnel, in material equipment, and in wealth, but also in the realm of theological education. The universities and theological schools of Europe have suffered so severely that they are not soon, if ever, fully to recover. In the British Isles the situation is not as grave, but the theological schools of the United States are presumably to have a much more prominent role in the future of Protestantism than they have in the past.

The mounting importance of the Protestantism of the United States means that the distinctive features of that Protestantism are to loom more largely in that wing of the world-wide Christian movement. These features are fairly familiar.

First of all, the left wing of Protestantism is relatively stronger in the United States than in Europe or even than in Great Britain. The Lutheran, Reformed, and Anglican Communions are prominent, but not so much so as on the other side of the Atlantic. They have lost most of the prestige which accrued to them in the Old World from being state churches. In the United States Baptists are the largest group, with Methodists second. Congregationalism is more to the fore than in England. A number of other bodies of the radical strain of Protestantism are represented. These, through their missions, for they usually are active in spreading their faith to other lands, are probably to add even greater world-wide strength to the extreme aspects of Protestantism.

This extreme Protestantism wishes to return to the Christianity of the New Testament and brands as corruptions all the subsequent developments. It regards with suspicion, therefore, the Catholic tradition and those features of Anglicanism and Lutheranism which perpetuate that tradition.

This does not mean theological "liberalism." That nineteenth- and early twentieth-century trend seems to be weakening. Much of the radical Protestantism of the United States tends to a conservative reliance upon the Bible and is suspicious of modern critical scholarship. In its more extreme forms it is Fundamentalism.

In the next place, in the United States a Protestantism is developing which is more varied and inclusive than is that of Europe. In the United States almost all the kinds of Protestantism exist that are to be found in Europe and the British Isles. They are there because they have been brought over by immigrants. To them have been added some of American origin. These different kinds of Protestantism live together on the basis of legal equality. They interpenetrate one another. Co-operation between denominations and the actual fusion of different communions have gone further in the United States than in Europe or even than in the British Isles.

Then, too, as in the Roman Catholic Church, so in Protestantism, the trend in the United States is toward activism, toward doing. The larger development of the "Social Gospel" in the United States than elsewhere is symptomatic.

Yet we must hasten to say that the Protestantism of the United States has produced and is producing first-class scholarship. Nor has it been sterile in creative theological thought. The leadership in both may pass to the United States, especially because of the impoverishment of Europe. That hegemony is not yet in evidence. The United States still looks expectantly across the Atlantic for theology, but, for better or for worse, it may begin to find itself disappointed and be driven to take refuge in its own resources.

The Protestantism of the United States has emphasized revivalism, special periods of appeal, often highly emotional, to win converts or to quicken the lukewarm. It is by this means that a large proportion of the mass conversion of which we have spoken has been achieved. The tendency seems to be away from this feature of American Christianity.

There has been, too, partly in contrast, emphasis upon what is often termed religious education. "Christian nurture" conducted from infancy in which the child shall grow up never thinking of himself as other than Christian has been stressed. It was to some extent a protest against revivalism but in practice the two have been combined.

In general the position of the United States has major implications for the future of all branches of Christianity. The United States is the wealthiest and in some respects the most powerful nation on the globe. How long it will continue to be so no one knows, but the present trend is to accentuate that position. We have been reminded until it has become a platitude that as the hundred years after Napoleon were the British century, so the coming ten decades or so are to be the American century. A contest is on between Russia and the United States. That, we must hasten to say, does not necessarily mean war, but the competition is there. In spite of palpable weaknesses, the United States has the advantage.

In the United States Christianity tends to be superficial. Much of the numerical growth of Christianity is at the expense of depth. Among church members there is an appalling religious illiteracy. As the proportion of church members in the population increases, the average of distinctively Christian living among them quite probably decreases. There is much of rampant secularism and either a quiet ignoring or a flagrant flouting of Christian principles of faith and conduct. Yet in the sense in which that term has been traditionally employed, the United States is predominantly a Christian nation.

These facts have at least three major corollaries. In the first place, the spread of Christianity will be more and more associated with the United States. In some quarters the wealth and prestige of the United States will assist in the expansion of the faith. In other quarters that expansion will be retarded, for opposition to the United States will take the form of opposition to Christianity. In the second place, the Christianity of the United States will tend to be more prominent in the world-wide forms of the faith. In the third place, since the Christianity of the United States is much more Protestant than Roman Catholic, Protestantism and Protestantism of the American type will mount proportionately to other forms in the entire Christian scene. All this may be good: it may be bad. More likely it will be a mixture of the two. But for better or worse it is the trend.

V

The British Dominions—Canada, Australia, New Zealand, and the Union of South Africa—have had such small populations that they will probably not loom large in determining the future trends of world-wide Christianity.

In Canada the aggressive and conservative Roman Catholic Church, mostly French but partly Irish, is rapidly increasing in numerical strength and is self-confident. Its growth is by an excess of births over deaths, chiefly because of the high birth rate of the rural French Canadians rather than through conversions. The latter are negligible. Canadian Roman Catholicism is local and has little effect upon the church as a whole. Except for the spilling over by immigration into the United States and for a small but growing number of foreign missionaries, it is confined to Canada. The Roman Catholic Church is not so prominent in any of the other Dominions. They are overwhelmingly Protestant.

The Protestantism of the Dominions is of a modified British

type. The two largest British communions, the Anglican and Presbyterian, prevail, with extensive bodies of Methodists, but with smaller percentages of Baptists and Congregationalists than in England. In Canada the fusion of the Congregationalists, Methodists, and a majority of the Presbyterians has partially altered the picture. In South Africa the Dutch Reformed Church is prominent. Although it is active in missions, this Protestantism of the Dominions is numerically so small a minority of the whole that probably it is not to have a major role in shaping the future of Protestant Christianity.

In general, so far as it has a share, the Christianity of the British Dominions will in large part reinforce the impulses given by that of the United States. It will make for the mounting place of Protestantism, and that mainly of Anglo-Saxon kinds, in the total Christian world scene. It is a less varied Protestantism and less weighted on the extreme left of that movement than is that of the United States, but it has kinship with it.

VI

Nor will Latin America count for much in the Christian global future. Its Roman Catholic Christianity is so passive that it must rely upon the faithful of other regions for missions to the pagan Indians on its own frontiers, and even, in part, for clergy for its old parishes. The latter are badly understaffed and much of the personnel is corrupt and incompetent. Very few missionaries go from Latin America to other lands. In some ways Latin America is more of a liability than an asset to the Roman Catholic Church. That situation is improving only slowly if at all.

Latin American Protestantism is more virile. It is growing rapidly, notably in Brazil. So far, however, it is dependent on the Protestantism of other lands rather than a contributor.

VII

Conditions in the world outside Europe, the Americas, and Australasia will obviously have effects upon the future of Christianity. Because the strength of Christianity and the material power of the world are still chiefly in these lands—the Occident in its largest sense—they will have the predominant share in the immediate future. Yet because of the recent rapid spread of Christianity throughout the earth and because the non-Occidental portions of mankind are in the majority we must take the latter into account.

First of all, we must note the effect of the growing restlessness under Occidental control. In some areas this means opposition to Christianity because of the latter's associations with the Occident. More generally it presages a continued increase of the rootage of the faith in other than the Occidental portions of the globe. The recent trend toward indigenous leadership in both Roman Catholic and Protestant circles and toward the autonomy of the "younger" churches of the Protestant wing of the faith will go on, probably at an accelerated pace.

There will be, too, especially in Protestantism, mounting impatience with the variations which had their origin in conditions peculiar to the Occident or to the history of one country in the Occident. This will intensify the movement toward cooperation and toward the actual union of different denominations. This we have already witnessed in a number of countries —notably in the South India United Church, in the Church of Christ in China, in the Church of Christ in Japan, and in the Philippines. In some of these movements toward union, missionaries rather than "nationals" have led, but in some, as in Japan, the demand for union has been primarily indigenous.

In Africa south of the Sahara the disintegration of the old

cultures and the swing toward Christianity have been so marked that if present trends continue we may expect professed Christians to be in the majority within the century. In the Union of South Africa those among the blacks who claim the Christian name are already more than half of the non-white population. The rapid increase in Equatorial Africa, especially in the Belgian Congo, Uganda, the Gold Coast, and Nigeria, seems to promise that within about two generations fully half the Negroes will have the Christian name. Much of this Christianity will be superficial. For many years the churches, as well as the political and economic life, will be under white supervision. Yet African initiative will grow. Among Roman Catholics, because of the structure of that church, control by the whites will long persist. Among Protestants, especially those of British and American connections, where the missionary emphasis has been toward the self-government of the churches, ecclesiastical independence will be hastened. This has been seen in South Africa. It will take forms which to the Occidental Christian will seem bizarre. The multiplication of native sects in South Africa and the prophet movements in some other parts of the continent may foreshadow a type of African Christianity of Protestant origin which will depart far from what has been known. Unfortunately one of the results seems to be a lowering of the average of Christian living. Mass conversion in Africa as elsewhere means superficiality and a Christianity which has the name but has in it much of superstition and is far from the standards of the New Testament. White direction through Roman Catholic and Protestant missions may help to approximation to the ideal, but it makes for an anemic and dependent Christianity which sags or succumbs when once the white man leaves. Growing independence of the African churches, as among British and American missions, is also accompanied by a decline which is initial but which may, by wise counsel rather than paternalistic direction, be reversed. One of the major problems of the world-wide Church for at least the remainder of the century will be this numerically growing but spiritually and morally infantile or adolescent African Christianity. The chief danger is a practical denial of the validity of Christian ethical standards and of the power of the Gospel to achieve them.

In the great central block of Islam which stretches from beyond the Straits of Gibraltar across North Africa into Western and Central Asia and, intermittently, across Southern Asia into the East Indies, there is little indication of any swing toward Christianity. The dwindling of the remnants of the pre-Islamic Christianity, the ancient churches of that area, now in progress for over a thousand years, continues. For instance, the Copts in Egypt annually lose to Islam several hundreds and even thousands. Roman Catholic and Protestant missions make their numerical gains almost entirely at the expense of these same churches. They usually bring a more vigorous Christian living and they have a few converts from Islam. They also leaven the lump of Moslem society with Christian ideals of character. But there is little indication of any extensive yielding of Islam to Christianity.

In India, Burma, and the East Indies the accessions to Christianity which have been so marked in the past few decades have been from underprivileged groups. The main body of the population, loyal to the traditional cultures and religions, has been little affected.

In India the Roman Catholic Church has its followers largely among the so-called "Portuguese." With only a slight admixture of Portuguese blood, they are in the Portuguese possessions and, scattered by migration, in some of the ports of India and the Far East. Their Christianity is fully as much a hallmark of proudly guarded communal "Portuguese" distinctiveness as of religious conviction. The Roman Catholic Church has also drawn tens of thousands from the "Syrian" Christian communities. Here and there, as in Chota Nagpur, it has had recent mass converts from the depressed classes and the animistic tribes. Protestantism has its numerical strength mainly in the depressed classes and the animistic tribes of primitive culture in the hills and jungles. Neither form of Christianity has drawn many from the dominant elements in the land, Islam and the Hindu castes. These elements have been touched, as through Gandhi. But, except here and there an individual or among the Sudras, they have not formally accepted Christianity.

In Burma the Christians are mainly from the Karens, before the advent of Christianity an animistic, despised enclave. The Burmese proper have been little affected.

In Ceylon Christians are about a tenth of the population, but most of them are Roman Catholics, descendants of converts of the days of Portuguese rule who came into the church as a matter of social and economic expediency.

In the Malay Peninsula the Christians are mainly among the Chinese element. This is now as strong numerically as the Malays, but the latter, Moslem for half a millennium, are almost entirely untouched. In Indo-China the large Christian gains are associated with French rule.

In the East Indies the Christians are predominantly from animistic primitive folk. The Moslem majority has lost only a few thousands to the Church. The large majority of the Filipinos are Christians, but the Filipino churches have shown no disposition to send missionaries to other lands. Only recently is the Roman Catholic majority being given Filipino clergy and bishops. It was a passive community, paternalistically governed by whites. The growing Protestant minority has more Filipino leadership and is concerned about spreading the Gospel within the islands, notably to the new settlements in Mindanao, but it is no more inclined to look beyond the borders of the islands to propagate its faith than are the Roman Catholics. The Filipino Independent Church, a secession from the Roman Catholics, is anemic spiritually. Its distinctive spirit is nationalistic, not religious.

In other words, the main numerical strength of Christianity in Southern Asia and the adjacent islands is in minorities who are apart from the dominant groups. It is to the glory of the Christian faith that it has "preached the Gospel to the poor" and has opened to them the door of opportunity to economic, intellectual, and spiritual advance. Moreover, the dominant cultures have been leavened by Christianity. However, Christianity has spread partly in connection with the economic, cultural, and political hegemony of the Occident. As white imperialism wanes, nationalism, whether Indian, Burmese, Singhalese, or Indonesian, will look askance at the Christian minorities as threats to national solidarity and to the continued control of the majority groups. In the decades immediately ahead, Christianity, whose growth has recently been so phenomenal in these areas, may, in part because of its very successes, encounter heightened opposition from the majority elements. These elements will be more and more in control of the governments and can reinforce their antagonism by political measures.

In China Christianity is less identified with one class or section than in any other land in Asia. It is to be found in every province. Naturally it is strongest along the coast, where the contact with the Occident has been longest and most intimate, and among those individuals who have been most exposed to Western culture. Yet, partly because of its very strength and its outstanding contributions, Christianity, and especially Protestant Christianity, has been stamped by conditions which must be temporary and by attitudes which partly caricature the Gospel. Because of the desperate political needs of China which arise from the prolonged revolution and the moral corruption in much of the leadership, many Christians have gone into the government through what was once the spearpoint of change and reconstruction, the Kuomintang. As that party has been longer in power much of its leadership has become corrupt and reactionary. The chief opposition is the Communists, who by tradition are anti-Christian. Christianity, and especially Protestant Christianity, tends to identification with the Kuomintang. Fortunately the identification is merely a trend. More subtle is the danger, partly from Confucianism and partly from aspects of Anglo-Saxon Protestantism, to value Christianity primarily as a means of social and political regeneration, and to test the value of the faith by its success in bringing unity and prosperity. This is not a complete misrepresentation of the Gospel, but it is clearly a distortion.

Korean Christianity is confronted in the North by the Russian Communist occupation. This comes on top of long-term Japanese hostility. The fate of the faith in all Korea depends in large part upon the political future of that unhappy land.

The Christianity of Japan has been partly Russian Orthodox, partly Roman Catholic, but chiefly Protestant. Orthodox Christianity has tended to follow the fortunes of the church in Russia and has suffered since the Russian revolution of 1917. The Roman Catholic Church has not been so intimately associated with political storms. Protestantism, however, has been introduced mainly from the United States and has spread chiefly among the urban professional and business classes, elements which have most nearly conformed to Occidental patterns. Therefore it suffered during the 1930's and the late war, for the reaction against the Occident and the hostility toward the United States were in part directed against it. Yet it has survived. Now the discrediting of the military through defeat in war has brought a more open-minded, even eager attitude. What the long-range effect of the American occupation will be cannot be known. It probably will be both favorable and unfavorable.

Set in a world of rapidly narrowing time-distances but of bitter antagonisms and kaleidoscopic changes, the present and future of Christianity are deeply affected. The strength of Christianity is still mainly in the Occident, but the decline of Western Europe and the passing of power to what was until recently the periphery of the Occident, Russia and the United States, are to have profound consequences. The weakening of the historic center of Christendom and the shifting of might eastward and westward are working changes which have only begun to be apparent but which are probably the early stages of long-term trends. Since Christianity is now world-wide it is to some degree conditioned by factors in every land. We have tried to indicate something of what is happening. We must now, in the next two chapters, attempt to describe the trends in each of the main branches of Christianity and to forecast the future. In looking into the future we cannot hope to foretell details. We can at best indicate the directions in which the currents are setting and suggest what, in broad outline, the results are to be.

CHAPTER VI

DIRECTIONS OF THE EASTERN CHURCHES
AND OF THE ROMAN CATHOLIC CHURCH

As WE come to the long-term trends in the main branches of Christianity a strange slow movement from east to west becomes apparent.

Christianity began on the eastern shores of the Mediterranean. It was there that Jesus lived, taught, died, and rose from the dead. It was there that the Church began. There almost all the books of the New Testament were written. Asia Minor was the first region of any size in which Christians constituted the majority of the population. Jerusalem and then Antioch, both in the East, were the earliest centers from which missionaries went forth. All the ecumenical councils of the first five centuries were held in the East.

With the rise and rapid spread of Islam in the sixth and seventh centuries the churches of the East began to dwindle. They were long vigorous. Nestorian Christianity all but spanned Asia through widely scattered minorities. The Monophysites flourished in Western Asia, Egypt, and Ethiopia. The Greek Orthodox Church won the peoples of the Balkans and became the dominant faith of Russia. Yet Islam slowly strangled some of the churches and dealt severe blows to the others. There was little overt persecution. Christianity was placed under disabilities but was tolerated. Where Moslem peoples were politically dominant the law of Islam was enforced. Conversions to Islam were possible but apostasy from Islam was punished by death. Christians could become Moslems, but Moslems could not become Christians. The churches showed persistent vitality, but, on the constant defensive, slowly gave ground. Through the capture of Constantinople by the Ottoman Turks in 1453 the citadel of Greek Orthodox Christianity passed into the possession of the followers of the Prophet and the cathedral church of that branch of the faith, St. Sophia, was transformed into a mosque.

With the triumph of Islam the main seat of Christianity moved to the western part of the Mediterranean. From the eleventh to the sixteenth century the Roman Catholic Church was the center of the most vigorous spiritual and intellectual life of Christianity. Through it the chief geographic extension of the faith was made from the sixteenth into the eighteenth century. The Russians held that Moscow was the "third Rome," succeeding Rome and Constantinople as the capital of true Christianity, but in vigor the Roman Catholic West surpassed anything that Russia or the East could display.

In the sixteenth century Protestantism arose in Northwestern Europe. From the outset it was vital and did more new things than any other of the contemporary branches of the faith. Yet until the nineteenth century it remained a distinctly and rather narrowly regional movement. Then it began rapidly to expand, much more so than the Roman Catholic or the Russian Church. Proportionately it is growing more than any other major wing of Christianity and for the next few generations the main stream of the faith will flow more and more through it.

In this westward movement of the center of Christian vigor there is nothing magical. "Westward the star of empire" is good rhetoric but it has nothing about it of inevitability. The stars do not fight in their courses for that slow transition.

The movement is entirely understandable. Part of it has been due, as we have said, to Islam. Part of it, as we suggested in an earlier chapter, is to be traced to the fact that the triumph of Christianity in the East was more apparent than real. The Roman state remained intact, kept the Church in a subordinate position, and prevented it from controlling culture as a whole. The nearer approach to collapse of the Roman Empire in the West challenged the Church to bring its faith to bear on all aspects of life and evoked more that was inherent in the Gospel. Christianity was freer to operate in the West. After the fall of Graeco-Roman culture it encountered the opposition of no high civilization. Supported by the prestige of Graeco-Roman culture of which it was the vehicle, it fairly easily won the able but barbarous people of the West. At the same time the fact that this was on the extreme western reaches of the Continent of Eurasia shielded the region from some of the conquests, such as those of the Arabs, the Mongols, and the Turks, which submerged the areas nearer the sources of invasion. When, in the sixteenth century, new life surged up in this Christianity, it found freest course in the Northwest of Europe. There the Roman Empire had either never reached or had been completely erased in the sixth and seventh centuries. There the ground was more fallow and the Gospel was less hampered in expressing its real genius. In the Southwest the Roman stereotype more nearly persisted and the religious awakening, although undoubtedly real, found vent through established and conventional forms and was, therefore, hampered and to some degree distorted.

Again as European peoples moved westward across the Atlantic they carried Christianity with them. In Latin America that was the Roman Catholic form of the faith and it was even more confined and controlled by the state than in Europe. It was, therefore, passive and tended to become corrupt in morals and sterile in spiritual force. In the British colonies Christianity was predominantly Protestant, it had representatives of most of the varieties of that form of the faith and so had much of its richness, and it was more nearly free from state control and more dependent on private initiative than anywhere in Europe. Its inherent power, therefore, flowered rapidly. Moreover, in nineteenth-century Britain state control declined, and the native vigor in Protestantism impelled individual Christians and groups of Christians to live their faith to the full.

I

The Eastern churches are apparently to dwindle. The shrinkage of those within Moslem lands continues, partly through losses of members to Islam, partly through conversions to Roman Catholicism or Protestantism, and partly through a slow decay in morale. This is true in secularized Turkey as well as in more loyally Moslem Egypt. The Gregorian (Armenian) Church has never recovered from the massacres and deportations of the nineteenth century and World War I and has been hampered by the Soviets. Nor have the Nestorian remnants regained what they lost in the tragedies of World War I. The Jacobites show little vitality and in Egypt the Copts, especially those in the villages, where almost no religious instruction is given them, are slowly being assimilated by the dominant Moslem community. The Ethiopian Church suffered from the Italian invasion.

The Orthodox churches can expect nothing but a long rearguard action against what may be progressive extinction.

The traditional center, the Patriarchate of Constantinople, which still jealously holds to the designation of Ecumenical, is in a pitiable condition. Only a few thousand Greeks in Turkey, mostly in Constantinople, are directly under it. The church in

Greece tends to side with it, for Greece and Turkey both fear Russia. Because of Russia and the strained Russo-Turkish relations, the churches in the Balkan countries under Russian influence can have little to do with it. Through Russian expansive ambitions, Turkey and the Soviets are probably to be chronically at enmity and the Ecumenical Patriarchate, a pawn in power politics, will face Russian opposition if it seeks to exert any influence over the Orthodox in the Soviet sphere.

The largest of the Orthodox churches, that in Russia, can probably not look forward to marked revival. Its resistance against the godlessness of the Soviet regime has been magnificent. It is now able to function more extensively than at any time since the Communists came to power. Yet aggressiveness on its part would quickly bring down upon it the censure and enhanced restrictions of the government. In none of its branches outside of Russia—in France, the United States, South America, and Japan—is there much evidence of vigorous life. The theological seminary in Paris, which for the years between the two wars gave indications of creative thought, seems not to have a hopeful future.

The Orthodox churches in the Balkans and Central Europe are in no better case. Not for several centuries have they displayed many movements which have been indications of renewed life. Here and there have been devoted, able leaders. Among the laity devout piety is still to be found. But the slow stagnation of the centuries has not been reversed. The long-term trends of which we have spoken which have made for the progressive sterility of the Orthodox churches have been strengthened rather than reversed. In Bulgaria, Rumania, and Greece the churches have put forth no new shoots in fresh monastic movements or theological thought. World War II dealt blows to what signs of new life had emerged before that cataclysm. The *Zoe* and *Aktines* movements in Greece are hopeful exceptions, but seem only to be exceptions.

The Orthodox churches will not soon die out. So far as one can see, they will live on for many centuries. In them are devotion and Christian faith which are too vital to be stifled even by the adverse conditions under which they exist. Yet the Orthodox churches are on the defensive. The future growth of Christianity must be looked for elsewhere.

II

The Roman Catholic Church is much more alive and not only displays vigor internally but is also expanding on its periphery. Yet if the future of Christianity were identified with that church the outlook would be grim.

The basic weakness of the Roman Catholic Church is that it is bound by its past. It is too much the ghost of the Roman Empire. It perpetuates the atmosphere of an age that is now gone and it is progressively less flexible. The Papal court with its ceremonial and dress is reminiscent of medieval or early modern monarchies and is an anachronism, although a picturesque and impressive anachronism. We must recall, too, how even the revival of the nineteenth century, marked though it was, predominantly took traditional forms. Not as much new was developed as in the emergence of the mendicant orders and the theology of the thirteenth century or even in the Society of Jesus in the sixteenth century. As it grows older the Roman Catholic Church does fewer new things and expresses fewer fresh ideas. That it glories in this as a sign of strength is evidence of weakness.

This trend has been present since at least the sixteenth century and rather than declining it has been reaffirmed and strengthened. In seeking to meet the Protestant Reformation the Roman Catholic Church through the Council of Trent defined its dogmas more precisely and in such fashion as to leave less room for flexibility of interpretation than had once been possible. It became less inclusive and more of a sect. While claiming universality it made of the word Catholic a party slogan rather than a designation which would embrace all Christians. Much more than before, the Roman Catholic Church became a distinct division within the Church of Christ.

Attempts to shake the Roman Catholic Church loose from this inflexibility or to stay its trend toward rigidity have proved futile. The protest against the drift toward Papal absolutism led to the expulsion of the dissidents and they were forced to form another sect, a small one, the Old Catholic Church. The attempt to enable the Roman Catholic Church to adjust itself to changing conditions by demonstrating that it had done so in the past was condemned as heretical modernism.

Moreover, it is significant that neither of these movements had in it much of spiritual dynamic. The church had become too stereotyped to be the womb of another such awakening as the Protestant Reformation or the Catholic Reformation. The church still possesses vitality, but not sufficient or at least not of the kind to give rise to a first-class heresy or a major reform. The turbulence of the Middle Ages and the Reformation, when the vitality in the church gave birth to many "heretical" groups, some of them large, which expressed profound religious conviction, has passed.

The Roman Catholic Church, it is almost gratuitous to say, has an enormous contribution to make to the Church Universal. Its loyalty to the incarnation of the Word in Christ, to the redemption wrought through the Cross, and to the hope and power of the life everlasting—to mention only some of the cen-

tral Christian affirmations to which it holds—gives its witness
continuing power. Its great minds through the ages, its wealth
of profound theological thought, the roster of its saints, the
wealth of its devotional and liturgical experience and literature,
and the long record of selfless devotion by many of its laity and
clergy possess an undying vitality for which all Christians of all
ages can be the richer. That life, fortunately, continues. The
Roman Catholic Church is still producing saints. Through it
millions are being nourished in the Christian life. The prayers
that thousands of its sons and daughters offer for their church
and the victory of its faith cannot go unanswered. God may and
probably will respond to those prayers in ways other than they
who utter them anticipate, but He will honor them.

Yet the Roman Catholic Church is too closely bound to a
past culture to be the continuing main channel of Christianity.
It is too Roman to be truly Catholic, in the sense of that word
which means universal. To be sure, it survived the collapse of
the Roman Empire, but it did so partly by utilizing and per-
petuating something of the machinery and the temper of that
state. It also outlived the death of Medieval Europe, but it carried over some of the luggage, irrelevant to the Gospel, which it
had acquired while helping to shape that period of Europe's life.

The Roman Catholic Church is a stranger in the present age.
As time goes on it will be more and more a stranger. The Gospel
is always at odds with its environment. True Christians are ever
pilgrims, seeking a homeland. But that homeland is not Rome.
The city of God has God for its builder and maker and is not, as
Augustine rightly saw, the counterpart or even the heir of any
earthly city. Even when the New Testament calls that city Jerusalem, it describes it as a new Jerusalem, coming down out of
heaven from God and not built on the physical or cultural foundations of the Judean city.

So far as the Roman Catholic Church is a stranger in the Christian sense it has an important witness to make. But it is a stranger partly in another than Christian sense. It is highly significant that its chief rootage has been and still is in that part of the world which was most assimilated to the Roman Empire and which was most Roman in its temper. This is Italy, France, Spain, Portugal, with parts of Switzerland, the southern and western banks of the Rhine, and the upper reaches of the Danube. The eastern shores of the Mediterranean were ruled by Rome, but in them the Romans were always conquerors and aliens. The perpetuation of the Roman Empire in Constantinople had a chronological continuity, but it was not really Roman in temper. In North Africa the Romans were powerful and built great cities, but in spite of over eight centuries of occupation were almost as much strangers as are the English in India after three and a half centuries. Britain was partly Romanized, but Roman rule and culture were effectively erased by the Germanic invasions. It was only Southwestern Europe which was fully assimilated to Rome. It is significant that the seat of the church is in Italy and in Rome itself. That fact is in theory accounted for by the presence in Rome of Peter, the chief of the Apostles, but this circumstance was adduced to justify the claims of the Church of Rome to absolute hegemony in the universal Christian fellowship.

Moreover, in the past four centuries the identification of the Roman Catholic Church with Italy and with Rome has been progressively heightened. Thereby the Roman Catholic Church has more and more been bound to one area and to the Roman tradition. In the Middle Ages the Popes were by no means all Italians. The Protestant movement led not only to the tightening of Roman Catholic dogma to that of a sect: it was also followed by the restriction of the Papacy to men of Italian birth and blood. Not for approximately four centuries has a non-Italian worn the tiara. For many generations the majority of the Cardinals were Italians and even the statesmanlike broadening of that college effected in 1945–46 has left the red hat on more Italians than upon the heads of any other one nationality. The large majority, too, in spite of the recent changes, are from Southwestern Europe—Italy, France, the Iberian Peninsula, South Germany, and Austria. The nineteenth-century affirmation of the dogma of Papal infallibility, the growth and dominance of ultramontanism, and the increasing centralization of the control of the church in the Vatican as against Gallicanism and other regionalisms and nationalisms, all make the church more Roman and more narrow. This control has been facilitated by the rapid communication of our day which enables administration of a world-wide organization to be carried on from one center. But this has simply hastened and made easier a trend which was already present. The Roman Catholic Church progressively reflects an era that has gone.

The identification of a church which claims universality with one cultural tradition and one segment of the world would be dangerous under any circumstances. It was not as much so when, as in the sixteenth, seventeenth, and eighteenth centuries, that section, especially through Spain, Portugal, and France, controlled a large portion of the earth's surface. Even in the nineteenth century, thanks to the new French colonial empire and to the holdover of the Spanish and Portuguese traditions in Latin America, the situation was not so obviously perilous. The majority of the nineteenth-century Roman Catholic missionaries were from France. In the twentieth century more missionaries are from France than from any other one country, but these come from the Roman Catholic minority, a minority which has continued to wane. Most of the other missionaries are from Italy, Germany, Austria, and Spain. The source of missionaries has spread, but it is still predominantly Southwestern Europe.

The shifting conditions of the present century have made the Roman tradition of the Roman Catholic Church peculiarly a liability. Much of Southwestern Europe has revolted from the church. That revolt was in progress in the eighteenth and nineteenth centuries. In the present century it has continued, and at an accelerated pace. The anticlerical movements, the secularization of much of the church property, and the separation of church and state in France have been phases of the rebellion. The large defections from the church, most of them more by a neglect or ignoring of the church than by overt attack, have been even more significant. On top of this revolt have been the blows dealt by the destruction through World War II and the permanent loss of world hegemony by Western Europe which we noted in an earlier chapter.

If we may try to put it in two sentences, the Roman Catholic Church is handicapped, probably permanently and increasingly, by being too closely bound to a particular cultural tradition and by being based primarily upon a small section of the globe. That section of the globe, through which it has mainly had its geographic extension, is now retreating from its four and a half centuries of dominance of the planet and is to have a declining role in world affairs.

Can the Roman Catholic Church make good its losses in Southwestern Europe by gains elsewhere? Can it live up to its aspirations and really be a world church? If so, the losses in Europe may be a blessing in disguise. They may force the church out of its narrow territorial and cultural grooves, shake it free from its provincialisms, and release its undoubtedly great inherent powers, powers derived from the Gospel itself, so that it can share and perhaps take the leading share in the next stage of the expansion of Christianity in the human scene.

At first sight the prospects for this development seem bright. The Roman Catholic Church is almost literally world-wide. It is the largest of all the Christian churches. Comparative statistics are uncertain, but it clearly has more adherents than all the Eastern churches combined and its members are probably more numerous than are all Protestants taken together. On much of its geographic periphery the Roman Catholic Church is growing rapidly. This, as we have seen, is strikingly the case in Equatorial Africa, the East Indies, Indo-China, and China, and to a less but still important extent is true in India. In other words, the Roman Catholic Church is a mounting if a minority factor in the greatest population masses outside the Occident. In all these lands, as we have said, it is becoming rapidly rooted through a growing indigenous priesthood and hierarchy and through the adaptation of Christian art to native forms. The Roman Catholic Church seems to be gaining in strength in the United States, one of the two most powerful and perhaps the most powerful of present-day nations. Some of the vast resources of that nation in personnel and wealth can, presumably, be utilized to redress the losses in Europe. Particularly can they be employed to replace the European staff and support of the world-wide missions of the church. Already the Roman Catholics of the United States are beginning to rise to the challenge. They are the chief source of the income of the Society for the Propagation of the Faith, an organization which is important in the financial undergirding of Roman Catholic missions. The Catholic Foreign Mission Society of America, still young, is recruiting, training, and sending to more and more countries a mounting number of extraordinarily able missionaries. The

American provinces of several of the standard orders, such as the Jesuits, the Franciscans, and the Society of the Divine Word, are increasingly taking responsibility for the missions of their respective bodies.

Then, too, the Roman Catholic Church already has a closely knit world-wide organization. While Protestants, handicapped by their many divisions, through the still embryonic Ecumenical Movement are groping their way to a global fellowship, the Roman Catholic Church has one which has long experience and which functions with an amazing degree of efficiency.

The present-day swing toward more power for the state seems to favor a church which stresses authority and which subjects its laity to its hierarchical priesthood.

Added to all this is what we have already mentioned and to which we will recur, the depth of spiritual life on the part of a potent minority and the striking loyalty of many of the laity and clergy and especially of the monastic orders and congregations. These latter, recruited from those who have given all to their faith, constitute a mighty force, disciplined, trained, obedient, convinced, devoted. Their members seem to be growing. Certainly in their new recruits the orders and congregations have increasingly a world-wide rootage, for these are more and more from the United States and non-Occidental peoples rather than, as until late in the last century, overwhelmingly from Europe. Here is a spiritual army, at its best trained in basic Christian beliefs, meditation, and prayer, and living selflessly for others in the service of Christ. A church so equipped is certainly not doomed to early extinction. Presumably it has a long and glorious future. On this as on the many other counts the Roman Catholic Church seems to have the promise of an enlarging place in the life of mankind.

Yet, as a more careful examination is given to the picture, the outlook for the Roman Catholic Church outside Europe is by no means as rosy as this optimistic summary would indicate.

First of all, we must note what we have hinted earlier, the liability of Latin America. The largest body of nominal Roman Catholics outside of Europe is in the Caribbean and on the mainland between the Rio Grande and Cape Horn. Here are the fruits of the major expansion of the Roman Catholic Church in the great period of missions begun by the age of discoveries and the Catholic Reformation. There are far more nominal Roman Catholics in Latin America than in all the rest of the earth outside of Europe, the United States not excepted. Yet this great body of Roman Catholics is more of a drag than an asset to the church. It does not have enough inner vitality to produce more than a handful of missionaries for the world mission. An examination of the roster of the total Roman Catholic missionary body by countries of origin discloses a pitifully small number from Latin America. Latin American Roman Catholicism does not provide enough missionaries to reach the pagan Indians on its own frontiers of mountain, jungle, and tropical valley. It does not have enough of its own clergy to care for its professed adherents within its own borders. Great parishes are left practically untended. Priests to staff the missions to the Indians have come from Europe and latterly from the United States. From the United States are also coming clergy to tend some of the parishes whose population for centuries has been professedly Christian. The testimony of these North American priests confirms what Protestants and some of the better Latin American clergy have long been reporting, the deplorable spiritual and moral conditions among the nominal Roman Catholics.

These conditions in Latin America are no recent phenomenon. They were aggravated by the complications which arose in the struggle for political independence. The adverse nineteenth-century factors which have operated in Latin Europe have also been present—anti-clericalism, secularism, and intellectual skepticism. Here and there has been slow improvement during the latter part of the last century and the present century. Yet the basic weaknesses go back to the planting of the faith in the region. Latin American Christianity has always been predominantly passive. In the colonial period the missionaries were mostly from Europe. The seculars and regulars from the American-born stock were chronically inferior. The church was paternalistically directed and controlled by the state.

The congenital weakness of the Roman Catholic Church in Latin America does not necessarily arise from the nature of that branch of the faith. In the United States and Canada, where, too, it was imported from Europe, the Roman Catholic Church is much more vigorous. The contrast may be due to the fact that in these two latter nations Roman Catholics have faced the competition of a Protestant majority. Yet this does not seem to be the secret, for in Brazil the rapid growth of a Protestant minority, largely by conversion from nominal Roman Catholics, has not stirred the Roman Catholic Church to a noticeable spiritual or moral revival. The cause appears to lie partly in the fact that the Roman Catholicism of Latin America was mainly from Spain and Portugal and partook of the faults of the church in those kingdoms, and partly because of the state paternalism through which it was introduced and governed. The colonial church in Latin America was much more closely controlled by the state than was the church in Spain or Portugal or, in a somewhat comparable deadening effect, the Orthodox churches of Eastern Europe.

Since no likelihood is to be found in Latin America for compensation for the losses of the Roman Catholic Church in Europe, does not the United States offer a more hopeful prospect? Here the answer must be an affirmative but a very qualified affirmative.

We have already noticed the mounting strength of the Roman Catholic Church in the United States and have called attention to the reasons for it. At the moment many Protestants are deeply concerned by that growth. Undoubtedly it is real. The wealth of the church is increasing by leaps and bounds. Some of that wealth is going to assist the church in Europe and missions on the far-flung frontiers of the church. Personnel in growing numbers is being recruited and trained for foreign missions.

Yet grounds exist for believing that the Roman Catholic Church is not far from the peak of its strength in the United States and that basic weaknesses forbid confidence that the losses in Europe will be fully redressed.

The reasons for holding that the Roman Catholic Church in the United States has about reached its peak and is probably to begin a slow decline as a factor in the nation's life are not far to seek. Some were hinted at in the preceding chapter.

In the first place, numerically as a proportionate part of the population the Roman Catholics are probably to decline. Immigration, the main source of the numerical gains, has been all but cut off since 1914. Throughout the history of the United States immigration had poured in chiefly from Europe. In the second two-thirds of the nineteenth century and in the twentieth century this had been increasingly Roman Catholic by tradition. The outbreak of World War I brought the flood to a sudden halt. After the war, when it might have been resumed, the Congress of the United States, in fear, passed restrictive legislation which put immigration on the quota basis. The quotas were so fixed as to encourage the coming of elements akin to the older

American stock. That stock was prevailingly Protestant, not Roman Catholic. Some Roman Catholic immigration still enters, but not enough to bring any large increase to the church.

Then, too, the Roman Catholic population is predominantly urban. This is because the immigrants, with nothing to offer except unskilled labor, found employment in the cities rather than in the rural districts. In the days of free land some went west, largely Germans, and took up farms. Most of the Roman Catholics settled in the cities of the Northeast and of the northern part of the Mississippi Valley. At the outset they tended to conform to their inherited European peasant patterns and to have large families. But urban conditions are unfavorable to a high birth rate. That of the urban Roman Catholics has, accordingly, been declining. The Irish, the source of much of the church's leadership in the United States, have especially been affected. This may be in part because they were the earliest large Roman Catholic national group in the United States and much more than the other early group, the Germans, found homes in the cities. Hence they have been longest subjected to urban conditions.

The Roman Catholic Church in the United States is, moreover, suffering numerically from the slow and unspectacular attrition of secularism. It maintains an extensive system of parochial schools, a magnificent effort to give its children education in a Christian atmosphere and, along with it, instruction in their faith. Yet thousands of Roman Catholic children attend the secularized public schools. The young people, among them some of the most intelligent, who have questions raised by what they have learned in the state schools which seem to them inconsistent with their faith, discard the latter and are lost to the church.

Many Roman Catholics become Protestants. This is not

through formal missions conducted for them. These have been singularly unsuccessful. Conversions have occurred chiefly as part of the process of assimilation to the life of the country. The United States is predominantly Protestant. Social prestige attaches to many of the Protestant congregations and attracts those wishing to be known as Americans. Numbers of Roman Catholics find the Protestant form of the faith and worship more congenial than that of the Roman Catholic Church. Some Roman Catholics become Protestants through marriage. How large is the leakage to Protestantism no one knows. No statistics are available. Yet quiet inquiry among Protestant pastors reveals the fact that it is not inconsiderable.

The Roman Catholic Church is attempting to compensate for these losses by reaching out to non-Catholics. The Paulists have long been active in missions to Protestants. In late years extensive efforts have been put forth in rural areas and among Negroes, both traditionally Protestant. These efforts are mounting. They are meeting with some success. Now and again a person of distinction in the political, business, or intellectual life of the nation becomes a convert and the accession is widely heralded. Many Protestants marry Roman Catholics and some of these become converts or promise that their children shall be reared as Roman Catholics. Again no comprehensive statistics are to be had. Presumably, however, the gains do not offset the losses.

So far as statistics are available, it seems probable that while the percentage of Roman Catholics in the population, like Christians in general, is increasing, it is not growing as rapidly as is the percentage of Protestants. Numerically, as compared with Protestants, Roman Catholics seem slowly to be losing ground.

Since the wealth of the Roman Catholic Church in the United States is mounting, for reasons which we suggested earlier, and since the church is impressive in size and is fairly closely knit, it will continue to be important. It will also contribute increasingly to the church as a whole. Yet there is no prospect that in material matters the Roman Catholic Church in the United States will fully make good the losses suffered in Southwestern Europe.

Ultimately the test will not be numbers or wealth but inner spiritual dynamic. It is this which is so largely lacking in Latin America. More of it is to be found in the church in the United States. As yet there is no indication of great fresh tides of life sufficient to revitalize and transform the church. The first and only American to be canonized was not born in the United States but in Italy. In this is a parable. Because of the youth of the church in the United States the time has not been sufficient for the slow processes by which the dead saints are officially recognized and raised to the altars. Yet there have been thousands of native-born Roman Catholics much older than this Italian-American saint and none of these has thus far been deemed worthy. Nor was the first saint from the Irish-Americans or the German-Americans who have dominated the church in the United States. The essence of canonization is that the person so honored is held up by the church as worthy of emulation by all Christians. Presumably thus far these stocks have not produced individuals who have had the kind of character which in the judgment of Rome can be so commended. This would seem to indicate that the Roman Catholics of the United States have not been distinguished for those qualities which their church itself deems pre-eminently Christian. Probably more will eventually be discovered. At present, however, the record is disappointing.

The Roman Catholic Church in the United States has displayed marked vigor in holding the majority of the immigrants of its faith and of their children. Through heroic efforts it has erected churches, schools, universities, theological seminaries, orphanages, and hospitals. It has recruited and trained priests. It has produced organizing ability. It has much of the conventional piety of the church. Its clergy are as a rule earnest and hard-working. Its monks and nuns are faithful. Its laity are more and more sharing in retreats and in the liturgical movement. But it seems slowly to be losing its hereditary constituency without fully making good the loss by fresh converts and it has not shown outstanding qualities in scholarship, in penetrating intellectual power, or, what is more important, in even the forms of Christian living traditionally esteemed by the church. Nor, still more significant, are there indications of fresh awakenings akin to those which produced the Cistercians, the Franciscans, the Dominicans, the Jesuits, or the Vincentians. The Roman Catholic Church in the United States is thus far a vigorous offshoot of the church in Southwestern Europe but without the qualities of genius and creative life which have marked that church at its best. There is no prospect that this wealthiest child of the Church of Rome will redress the losses suffered by its mother. In this, as we shall see, the situation in Protestantism is far different.

If Latin America and the United States cannot make good the losses of the Roman Catholic Church in Europe, is there hope elsewhere? Numerically these lands contain the main bodies of Roman Catholics outside of Europe. The other groups are smaller. In Canada the leaders of the church are confident and aggressive. Because of the high birth rate, particularly of the French elements, the Roman Catholic Church is growing more rapidly than the Protestants and within a generation or two may outnumber them. Yet the Canadian church is conservative and gives no indication of any striking awakening. Nor is it to assume numerical proportions comparable to those of the church in Latin America or the United States.

There is even less indication of new life in the Roman Catholic Church in the other British Dominions.

In several parts of the non-Occidental world the church is, as we have seen, growing rapidly in numbers and leadership. In none of these, however, is it fully independent of white supervision. Nor in any of them are there fresh tides of life which are spreading to the Occident and revitalizing the faith. Probably they cannot be expected from a church as inflexible and stereotyped as is that of Rome.

We must note, moreover, that the seeming unity of the Roman Catholic Church is deceptive. At first sight it appears to presage the unity which is desperately needed in our modern world and to be a realization of what divided Protestantism is groping toward in its Ecumenical Movement. For certain purposes the Roman Catholic unity is real. It carries with it agreement in creed and submission to a central authority in matters of faith and morals. However, if true Christian unity be that of love the Roman Catholic Church does not possess it. Orders are jealous of one another. Bishops jockey for power. National feeling is strong. The Pope may speak in noble words of the high principles which should govern international relations, but they have little if any practical effect in preventing or stopping wars in which Roman Catholics are on opposite sides. If one accepts the Roman Catholic basic postulate that for the eternal salvation of souls acquiescence in a particular creed and the validity of certain sacraments are essential, the Roman Catholic Church has unity. But if one longs to see that unity demonstrated now in present, inclusive brotherhood, the Roman Catholic Church is fully as deficient as is Protestantism. Indeed, Ecumenical Protestantism has already in its brief course done more to preserve the ties of understanding between Christians in various nations and to effect reconciliation after war than has the Roman Catholic Church. It has made more progress toward bridging and closing the gulfs in its own ranks, although these are still great, than has the Roman Catholic structure the chasms which exist within its fellowship.

Nor is there the slightest possibility that the Roman Catholic Church will attract all Christians to its fold. As we have suggested, it has never embraced "all those who profess and call themselves Christians." The Christians outside its fold increase rather than diminish. Here and there, in lands where the church is a minority set in a Protestant majority, notably in the United States, some fraternization occurs. The National Conference of Christians and Jews is an example and a channel. Yet the lines which officially separate the Roman Catholic Church from other Christian bodies are more and more tightly drawn. That church will not attract large numbers of other Christians to its fold. Even now, in Latin America and the Philippines, it is losing more members to Protestantism than it is gaining elsewhere from all other Christian bodies. Nor will Rome ever consent to co-operation with other churches on the basis of equality. It will never join a world council of churches.

The Roman Catholic Church is not dying. If the planet and the human race last that long, it will go on for untold centuries. It will even continue to spread geographically. For millions it will be the authority in religion. Yet as a factor in world affairs it probably has reached or passed its peak.

The Roman Catholic Church seems to be at about the place where Buddhism was a thousand years or so ago. Like Buddhism of a millennium since, it possesses hoary antiquity; it appeals to millions; it is to be found in many nations; it continues to spread geographically; it still has marked spiritual vitality. But it is weakening in the land of its origin; it is becoming stereotyped; and it is ceasing to give rise, as it once did, to new and creative currents of life.

The parallel with Buddhism is by no means exact. The Roman Catholic Church is spread more widely geographically than Buddhism ever has been. A longer time has elapsed since the beginning of Christianity and the Church of Rome than had intervened between the Buddha and the state of Buddhism which we have compared with the present condition of the Roman Catholic Church. The decline in the latter is much less pronounced than it was in Buddhism ten centuries ago. It is possible that a fresh surge of life will once more bring a new day for the Roman Catholic Church.

Yet the parallel with Buddhism is sufficiently close to be sobering. In each case a great religious system is born, prospers, becomes stereotyped, slowly stagnates, and still more slowly but still surely loses ground.

If the future of Christianity depended upon the Eastern churches or the Roman Catholic Church, the prospect would be discouraging.

CHAPTER VII

DIRECTIONS IN PROTESTANTISM

FORTUNATELY for Christianity Protestantism offers far more hope for continued growth and expanding vitality than do the Eastern churches or even the Roman Catholic Church.

I

At first sight this seems not to be true. Some of the weaknesses which we have noted in the Roman Catholic Church appear also to be found in Protestantism and to these are added others from which the Roman Catholic Church is thought of as being free. Protestantism also seems to be tied to a particular culture which is dying and to an area of the earth's surface which is diminishing in importance.

Protestantism appears to be largely a religion of the middle class and to be associated with a type of individualism which is passing. In much of Western Europe its strength was in the middle class. Some of what it has stressed as virtues have been traditionally associated with middle-class industry, thrift, and personal responsibility. Its emphasis on salvation by faith and the priesthood of all believers tends toward a kind of rugged individualism which rejects all autocratic restraints and which has kinship to the *laissez faire* and absence of government control which characterized the Occident in the nineteenth century. From this viewpoint it is understandable that the nineteenth century should be the "Protestant century" and that in it that form of the faith should spread relatively more rapidly and flourish more vigorously than did even Roman Catholicism. However, in our day the middle classes are suffering and are being ground between the upper and nether millstones of a rising proletariat and augmented state domination. Inflation and high taxes press on them harder than on some other groups. *Laissez faire* is outmoded, although in the United States it is only slowly retreating, fighting a rear-guard action.

Protestantism had its origin in Northwestern Europe and until the close of the nineteenth century its main strength lay there and in Great Britain. Indeed, down into the present century most of its creative thought has been in that area. This area, like Southwestern Europe, is declining. Even Great Britain is not to be as prominent as it was in the nineteenth century.

Protestantism is, too, receiving severe blows in its traditional seat, much as the Roman Catholic Church is doing in Latin Europe. Defections and persecutions have cost it dear.

The doctrinal content of Protestantism appears to be weakening as that of the Roman Catholic Church is not. Large elements of Protestantism seem to be departing from the historic Christian faith. Attempts to make peace with the modern temper and the scientific attitude have led to a kind of liberalism which ignores or denies some of the main tenets to which the vast majority of Christians have always held. Many, both Roman Catholics and Protestants, hold that the basic convictions of Christianity are slowly leaching out of Protestantism, that the salt is losing its savor.

These alleged weaknesses are most speciously set forth, sometimes by critics outside Protestantism, sometimes by Protestants themselves. That the charges possess elements of truth is incontrovertible.

II

However, the weaknesses are not so prominent or so widespread as might at first sight be supposed. It is a mistake to identify Protestantism with the middle class. To be sure, it has been strong in that class. Yet it has also been and is well rooted in other classes. In much of Germany, in Scandinavia, in Scotland, and among the majority in England it has by tradition been the faith of the community—of all, both high and low. In the United States it has been, so far as those elements have had a faith, the predominant religion of the older stock, both white and black. It has been stronger in the rural districts and in the small towns, where this stock prevails, than in the big cities where class lines are more sharply drawn.

Moreover, although Protestantism is closely associated with democracy, that form of political organization and that temper of society are not moribund nor do they necessarily mean *laissez faire*. Democracy is having hard going, but it is still spreading.

We must also point out that Protestantism is not so nearly identified with Western Europe as is Roman Catholicism. It has long been dominant in Great Britain and that island has suffered less than has the neighboring Continent. Then, too, Protestantism is far stronger in the United States than is the Roman Catholic Church. It is growing there more rapidly, both in total numbers and in proportion to the population. The culture of the United States is much more closely associated with Protestant than with Roman Catholic Christianity. The outstanding position held by the United States in the world makes, therefore, for the strengthening of Protestantism.

As to the denaturing of Protestantism by an easygoing and compromising liberalism, that diagnosis is a caricature. Like all caricatures it has elements of truth, but it is a distortion and not an accurate picture. Much of this "liberalism" is an evidence of vigor. It betokens a flexibility which, while insisting on the basic features of the Christian faith, shows that these essentials are not inconsistent with what modern scholarship has disclosed about the nature of the universe and of man. Indeed, the best of Protestant thought is stating with marked cogency the striking pertinence of the Christian faith to our era.

III

More important as evidence that the main stream of Christianity is moving through Protestantism and that, when Protestantism is considered, Christianity is clearly not dying out, are a number of positive considerations.

First of all, the spread of Christianity is now proportionately more through Protestantism than through the Roman Catholic Church. That was true in the nineteenth century. It is true today. In some areas, as in the Belgian Congo where Roman Catholic forces are concentrated and have the support or at least the sympathy of the government, the reverse is the case. Roman Catholics are mounting at a quicker pace than are Protestants. So, too, in Uganda and Kenya, although for different reasons, the Roman Catholic increase is more marked than is that of the Protestants. Yet in Nigeria and the Gold Coast the opposite is true. In the Netherlands East Indies on the eve of World War II, measured by percentages the Roman Catholic minority was gaining more rapidly than the Protestants who constituted the majority of the Christians. But in India Protestants have been increasing faster than Roman Catholics. In China, although, because they have been there more than twice as long, Roman Catholics far outnumber Protestants, their percentage of growth seems not to be as great as that of the latter. Statistics for China since the Japanese invasion are too uncertain to enable us to know precisely what is happening in totals of Christians. But the figures on the eve of that invasion showed the recent percentage increase of Protestants to be larger than that of Roman Catholics. Certainly that was the case in the latter part of the nineteenth and the fore part of the twentieth century. In the United States, as we have said more than once, the Protestants are numerically more of a majority as against the Roman Catholics than they were in 1914. It is significant that in some nominally Roman Catholic populations Protestants are making far larger inroads than are Roman Catholics in any professedly Protestant constituency. This is seen in Latin America, especially in Brazil and Mexico, and to a lesser extent in all the republics. In the Philippines, in their Roman Catholicism closely related to Latin America, Protestantism is also growing rapidly.

In the second place, and more important than the numerical count, is the fact that the world-wide influence of Christianity upon the contemporary scene has been more through Protestantism than through any of the other forms of the faith. In the Occident the contribution of Christianity to the formation of the League of Nations and then to the United Nations has been mainly through Protestantism. One need here merely cite the outstanding role of Woodrow Wilson in bringing the League of Nations into being and the place, not so outstanding but still important, of another Protestant layman and of a Protestant clergyman in the framing of the Charter of the United Nations. In China, although Roman Catholics have been continuously represented over twice as long and for that reason greatly outnumber Protestants, it is the latter who exert far the largest nation-wide influence. It has been Protestant schools, Protestant medical and public health efforts, and Protestant initiative in improvements in forestry and agriculture which much more than Roman Catholic efforts have contributed to the new education, medicine, public health, forestry, and agriculture. Sun Yat-sen was a Protestant, not a Roman Catholic, and the overwhelming majority of the Christians who have been prominent in the government of the Republic have been Protestants. The channel by which the New Testament came to Gandhi was Protestant, not Roman Catholic, and so the effect which Christianity has had upon India through him has been of Protestant mediation. Most of the depressed classes of India who have entered the Christian faith have come into Protestant churches. The unrest among these groups, therefore, is more of Protestant than of Roman Catholic derivation. The effect of Christianity upon the general life of Japan has been almost entirely through Protestantism and the most prominent Japanese Christian, Kagawa, is a Protestant. That reduction of languages to writing which has been so marked a result of Christianity in the past century or more and which still continues has been chiefly by Protestants.

In the third place, the rooting of Christianity among non-Occidental peoples has probably proceeded further in Protestantism than in the Roman Catholic Church. The latter has thus far been more successful in recruiting and giving a prolonged training to an indigenous clergy than has the former. Roman Catholic Christianity has emphasized the Church and is building a well-integrated Christian community. Protestantism has had greater influence upon non-Occidental society as a whole but has not yet given rise to as highly articulated a Christian community. That is in part because it is more this-worldly, places less emphasis upon the sacraments, and is ecclesiastically more divided. Yet Protestants have by no means failed in producing an indigenous clergy, nor are they by any means wholly this-worldly. In national and regional organizations such as the National Christian Councils of India and China, indigenous leadership has more authority than in comparable Roman Catholic bodies. In the case of some, notably Japan, complete administrative independence from the Occident has been achieved. Several of the other churches founded outside the Occident by Protestants are, too, independent of control by Occidental bodies. This is nowhere true of the Roman Catholic Church.

This indigenization of Protestant bodies would be dangerous were it not for the Ecumenical Movement. Apart from the Ecumenical Movement these several national organizations or local independent bodies would tend to subordinate themselves to the purposes of the peoples among whom they are set. Or they would conform to the cultures about them to the sacrifice of principles essential to the Gospel. Some of them have not entirely resisted these temptations. Yet by the rapid growth of the Ecumenical Movement they are being more and more consciously bound into the world-wide Christian fellowship. Non-Occidentals have been and are prominent in several of the organizations which go to make up the Ecumenical Movement. Non-Occidentals are much more in evidence in these Protestant ecumenical bodies than they are in the central structure of the Roman Catholic Church.

In the fourth place, this Ecumenical Movement, that novel effort to bring Christians together to meet the needs of mankind on a global basis, is, as we have more than once reminded ourselves, of Protestant origin.

It is significant that the stereotyped and traditional method of attaining Christian unity which is embodied in the Roman Catholic Church has not succeeded in attracting all Christians. Here and there, as in the case of several thousands from the Syrian Church of India, it has recently won accessions. These, however, have been more than offset by secessions such as the Russian-engineered loss of the Ruthenian Uniates and the older (but still in the present century) separation of the Polish National Catholic Church of America and the resumption of connection with the Orthodox Church by thousands of Rumanian Uniates in the United States.

The Ecumenical Movement is, by contrast, through new approaches. It does not require the full conformation of its members to a central authority. It permits and even encourages more variety than does the Roman Catholic Church. Indeed, that variety is already much greater than the latter has ever displayed. It includes not only representatives of almost all the main ecclesiastical families of Protestantism. In one way and another it also has drawn in Old Catholics, some of the Orthodox and other Eastern churches, and even, in more than one of its phases, has succeeded in obtaining the co-operation of a few Roman Catholics. It has brought in these non-Protestants not with the purpose of making them Protestants, but with the desire for larger and more inclusive fellowship and achievement. A movement which is both new and growing is evidence of abounding life and of youthful resilience and adaptability. Such ability to reach out in fresh ways is extraordinarily hopeful for the future.

IV

These four indications of the vigor of Protestantism, as against the other kinds of Christianity, do not prove conclusively that Christianity will go on through this branch. Numerical growth, effect upon the total human scene, indigenous non-Occidental leadership, and new ways in which Christian unity is being achieved are important. They are clear evidence of a life within Protestantism which augurs well for the future. Yet they are hopeful chiefly as evidence of an inner vitality which issues from the eternal Gospel. The future of Protestantism as of Christianity itself rests primarily upon the degree to which these inward springs of transforming power are allowed free course.

At present Protestantism is not displaying markedly any of the fresh tides of life which have traditionally been manifestations of that inner power. We seem to have nothing equal to the Pietist or Moravian movements of the seventeenth and eighteenth centuries, to the Great Awakening and the Second Awakening which swept across the nascent United States, to the Evangelical revival associated with the names of Wesley and Whitefield, or to those revivals which had Charles G. Finney and Dwight L. Moody as their successive leaders. Nor do we have movements which create as much opposition as did the early Quakers.

The apparent lack of such upsurges of the Spirit may, however, be from a faulty perspective on our part, from insensitiveness to what is happening before our eyes, or from an insistence that future awakenings within Protestantism must follow the patterns of their predecessors. It is conceivable that, seen from the vantage of a later generation, some of the movements within Protestantism of our day will prove to be quite as epoch-making as the earlier ones which we have mentioned. If so, the very fact that they are not following precedents will be an indication of vigor. The unwillingness to conform to historical stereotypes, in striking contrast with Eastern and Roman Catholic Christianity, may be additional evidence that the main current of the faith is more and more through Protestant channels.

Among the features of Protestantism which may be so adjudged by those who come after us are the pacifism which has caught up ardent and loyal minorities, the extensive works for the relief of the suffering produced by war, renewed hunger for the inner life of the Spirit, the Confessional Church in Germany, Sigtuna in Sweden, the Iona Community in Scotland, some kindred fellowships in the United States, and the Ecumenical Movement. Certainly a branch of Christianity which is putting forth so many robust new shoots is very much alive.

V

The Protestantism of the future will not be the Protestantism of the past. We cannot yet clearly discern what that Protestantism is to be. We can, however, perceive something of the direction which is being taken and from it may be able to forecast in part what is to come.

The very fact that we cannot foretell the precise or even the general features of the Protestantism of the future is probably evidence of vitality in that branch of Christianity. We can be fairly safe in the conjecture that the Eastern churches—such of them as survive—and the Roman Catholic Church of a century or two centuries hence will not be substantially different from what they are today. Their patterns have been so constant for so many generations that, in the case of the Eastern churches, they will be maintained without substantial alterations, and, in the Roman Catholic Church, they will be preserved and the progressive strengthening of the Papacy and its control of the church will be accentuated. Protestantism, however, is not so stereotyped. It is still flexible. If it can maintain and strengthen its allegiance to the Gospel and its professed Master, this characteristic of being unfinished, of still being adjustable, can be of great advantage and a means to continued growth. If its wineskins are sufficiently new to hold the eternally fresh wine of the Gospel, Protestantism will endure. If its wineskins harden, then the Gospel will break out from them and another form of Christianity, now quite undiscernible, will succeed it and in turn become the main expression of the faith.

We have already reminded ourselves that, as a description, Protestantism is a misnomer. Here is a kind of Christianity which is a continuation of the historical stream but which is as distinct as any of the Eastern churches or the Roman Catholic Church. The fact that it is so varied is one of its characteristics. The wide range of today from the Friends and Baptists on the one hand to the Lutherans and the Anglicans on the other is an authentic feature which goes back to the first century of Protestantism. Yet in spite of the variety there has been a basic unity in Christ, in salvation by faith, and in the priesthood of all believers. Protestantism is a fresh yet old kind of Christianity.

May we describe the trends in the Protestantism of our day and so attempt to discern what the Protestantism of the decades immediately ahead is to be? If we are right in our analysis, if the main current of Christianity is flowing more and more through Protestantism, then in these trends we are to see something of the Christianity of the future.

First we must remind ourselves again that in Protestantism the influence of the Continent of Europe and even of the British Isles is waning and that that of the United States is increasing. This, obviously, is because of the decreasing weight of the first two and the mounting power of the last in world affairs.

This means a decline in the position of Lutheranism in Protestantism. The commanding place in Protestant thought held by Lutheran scholars in the nineteenth century is probably not to be repeated. Lutheranism will not disappear. It continues in Germany and Scandinavia and some of its leaders carry weight throughout Protestantism. In the United States Lutheranism is numerically strong and its churches show initiative. Creative thought is still emerging, notably in Sweden. Yet in the United States the Lutherans are a minority, although a substantial minority. Most of them, too, are by their own choice largely cut off from the co-operative enterprises which characterize the Protestantism of the dominant Anglo-Saxon tradition and so do not carry as much weight as they might were they fully in them.

We must remember, moreover, that Lutheranism is suffering not only from the decline of Western Europe but also from the weakening of the churches in Germany wrought by the adverse conditions of the present century, especially secularism and National Socialism.

We must note, too, that in the Lutheranism which persists confessionalism is strong. The liberalism and radicalism of some strains of nineteenth-century Lutheranism have faded in the harsh world which surrounds European Lutheranism. The majority of American Lutherans, especially those of the nineteenth-century immigration, are extremely conservative and have not yet yielded to the currents of liberalism found in some of the surrounding Anglo-Saxon Protestantism.

The waning of Anglicanism which will follow the decline of Great Britain will, like that of Lutheranism, be only relative and will not be nearly so marked as that of the latter. Britain is still prominent and will continue to be so for an indefinite future. The Church of England will share its prominence. The Anglican Communion is much stronger in the British Dominions and in the British Empire in general than is Lutheranism. It is also more widespread in China, India, and Japan, lands which are to loom large in the future. In the United States it is not so strong numerically but it is more closely associated with the main stream of Protestantism and of the culture of the country and so has more effect upon them. Anglicanism is having a large and probably a growing influence upon much of the Protestantism of the "free churches."

Yet Anglicanism cannot escape the weakening of the world position of the British Isles. In England it has, too, suffered from the mass defections which we have noted as one of the features of current English life.

Protestantism of the Reformed tradition is not to suffer as severely as Lutheranism and probably not so much as Anglicanism. It is not so centered on the Continent of Europe as is Lutheranism, and, in general, it has been more resistant to the adverse conditions than has this other main form of Continental Protestantism. Marked vigor is apparent in the Reformed churches in the Netherlands, Germany, Switzerland, and France. The Church of Scotland is also sturdy and in it has arisen the Iona Community, evidence of a life that can create something new. Moreover, in the United States and the British Dominions the Reformed and Presbyterian churches are very strong. They have, too, long been active in sending missionaries to the non-Occident, and in Africa, the Near East, India, the Netherlands East Indies, the islands of the Pacific, the Philippines, China, Korea, and Japan churches of the Reformed tradition are prominent. In some areas, as in South India, China, and Japan, they have become nuclei of union movements which have drawn in other denominations. They are more nearly in accord with the prevailing currents in the rest of Protestantism than are the Lutherans or even the Anglicans.

In the next place, the strain in Protestantism which is growing most rapidly is what in England is called the "free churches." These represent the extreme wing of Protestantism and are those which have stressed most salvation by faith and the priesthood of all believers. They do not, as do the Lutherans and the Anglicans, prize much of what developed in the Catholic Church of the Roman Empire and its successors. They are more nearly thoroughgoing than are the Reformed churches in their resolution to return to the New Testament and to regard as corruptions of the Gospel all developments in organization, worship, and creeds between the first century and the emergence of their own particular denomination.

The growing strength of this extreme wing of Protestantism is due to a variety of factors. One is the obvious fact that this wing has been only slightly represented on the Continent of Europe. There the Lutheran and Reformed churches were so emphatically supported by the state that the more radical Protestant groups were almost entirely stamped out. The adverse effect upon them of the weakening of Western Europe has, accordingly, been slight. They have traditionally been vigorous in England and the awakening of the nineteenth century greatly reinforced them in that land. Along with the Church of England they have suffered from the weakening of the world position of Great Britain and from the failure to win the allegiance of millions of the rising generation. Yet they are still potent. Except for Methodism they are not nearly so prominent in the British Dominions as in England.

The outstanding place held in the United States is the chief reason for the growth of influence of these radical forms of Protestantism. In the early days of the settlement of that land they achieved a prominence which they have never lost. Their place in the founding of New England, Pennsylvania, and New Jersey is well known. They flourished in the opening years of the new republic. They were peculiarly successful in following the westward moving frontier and became the prevailing faith of the pioneers. The awakenings and revivals which were characteristic of the religious life of the United States of the eighteenth and nineteenth centuries fed into them more than into the other branches of Protestantism. More of the older American stock, both white and black, is to be found in them than in all the other forms of Protestantism and of the Roman Catholic Church put together. From their exuberant life issued foreign missions. As a result, partly of the missions of the "free churches" of England but more because of the missions of the Baptists, Methodists, Congregationalists, and others of the extreme forms of Protestantism found in the United States, the "younger churches" of Protestantism in most non-Occidental lands are much more of this complexion than in the Continent of Europe and more even than in England. The mounting place of the United States in the twentieth century will strengthen this element in Protestantism. That will be seen in non-Occidental lands, where missions from the United States will be proportionately much more prominent than in the past. It will be notable in the total numerical world strength of Protestantism. It will also be witnessed in the leadership in worldwide Protestantism. Within the past ten years the secretariat of the International Missionary Council has shifted from members of the Reformed churches to this wing of Protestantism. The ecclesiastically somewhat more conservative World Council of Churches is still predominantly in Reformed, Lutheran, and Anglican hands, but that is because this body is concentrating its efforts on the Continent of Europe. In the United States the support for the World Council of Churches is more from extreme Protestantism. For instance, both the chairman and the secretary of the American Committee for the World Council of Churches are at this writing Congregationalists.

The prominence of extreme Protestantism in the United States and the "younger churches" of the non-Occident makes for at least three other trends in world-wide Protestantism. One is the tendency to discount what might be called the "Catholic" tradition, namely, those features of Christianity which were shaped in the dominant church of the Roman Empire and were further developed in the Roman Catholic Church in Western Europe before the Reformation. We have seen why these are so largely rejected by radical Protestantism in the Occident. In the non-Occident some of the leaders wish to strip Christianity of its Occidental accretions and to acclimatize it to the local environment. While a few radicals, especially in India and Japan, have espoused this view, the bulk of the non-Occidental Christians have not followed them but have held to what has been transmitted to them from the West. Yet a tendency exists to be impatient with Occidental sectarian divisions and not to hold as tenaciously as Westerners to convictions which lie back of particular denominations.

Another trend in Protestantism which springs from the radical wing and which is akin to the slighting of the "Catholic" tradition is the weak consciousness of the Church as a comprehensive and unique institution. For Occidental Protestants this arises partly from a reaction against the Church as represented by the Roman Catholic Church and by some Protestant churches which, supported by the state, have persecuted dissidents. It also springs from the individualistic character of extreme Protestantism with its emphasis upon the salvation of each Christian through the faith of that Christian and to a form of ecclesiastical polity in which the local congregation is the "church" and is self-governing and in theory independent of every other congregation. For non-Occidental Protestants there is added the factor that nothing quite like the Church is to be found in the inherited religions with which they are familiar. The Church is a unique creation of the Christian faith and time is required to develop a conception of it and loyalty to it.

Partly through the Ecumenical Movement a consciousness of the Church as inclusive of all Christians and possessing a long history is growing among many of the leaders of radical Protestantism in the United States. This is probably to increase.

A third effect of extreme Protestantism is to reinforce a trend to regard the Christian community as a minority set in a hostile world. That trend is already strong among other Protestants. It is also seen among Roman Catholics. The reasons are probably to be found partly in the nature of the Gospel, partly in the defections in the Occident and the outspoken hostility of some of the new ideologies, and partly in the fact that in spreading in the non-Occident, as it has been doing rapidly of late years, Christianity has so far appealed, for obvious reasons, only to minorities and to some of those from underprivileged groups who have a self-conscious inferiority. This trend, so widespread in Christianity, is especially strong in the radical Protestantism which stresses the conversion of the individual and, as a corollary, a manner of life which is sharply distinct from that of non-Christians. In the United States the trend is partly obscured by the mass conversion which, as we have said, is in progress. The mounting percentage of church members in the population, largely in the growth of such radical denominations as the Baptists and Methodists, means a watering down of the requirements for church membership and an increasing fuzziness of the line which separates Christians from the world about them.

Still another effect of extreme Protestantism upon future Christianity, in partial contradiction to this last, is to stress the place of Christianity in transforming all of society. Much of Anglo-Saxon and especially of American Protestantism tends to be activistic, to be intent upon bringing all of human culture into conformity with Christian ideals. This trend has been regarded with suspicion by much of the Protestantism of Europe.

It has been seen in the strong movement in the Protestantism of the older American stock to work for peace and to make the voice of the churches heard in international affairs. Since American Protestantism is growing in total Protestantism and, therefore, in Christianity, we may anticipate increased effort in this direction.

Another marked tendency in Protestantism is, as we have said, to the unity of Christians, to co-operation across denominational lines, and, in some instances, to the ecclesiastical union of previously distinct bodies.

This trend is particularly marked on the newer geographic frontiers of Christianity and among radical Protestants. On these frontiers the transmitted ecclesiastical patterns have less reason for existence than in the areas where they originated and have had time to solidify. They are, therefore, viewed with impatience. Since in the nineteenth and twentieth centuries the expansion of Protestantism has been rapid, the trend toward unity has been accelerated. It has become prominent in the United States in the Protestantism of the older white stock, where denominations have long existed side by side, have interpenetrated one another, and have faced together their common tasks. It is seen in the United Church of Canada, which was forced on the churches in the older parts of the Dominion by conditions in the newly settled West. The Church of Christ in Japan, the Church of Christ in China, and the Church of South India are other pertinent examples. The tendency is being accelerated almost by geometrical progression.

A corollary of this movement toward co-operation and union which constitutes another feature of contemporary Protestantism is the trend toward national Protestant bodies which embrace all Protestant Christians within a given country. This is seen, to select only a few examples, in the National Christian Councils of India and China, the Federal Council of the Churches of Christ in America, and the British Council of Churches. Thus far none of these bodies is as tightly knit as are the historic state churches. None is allied to the state and none persecutes those Christians who do not join them. All permit large variety within and without their ranks and are co-operative undertakings of reciprocally independent ecclesiastical bodies. The tendency is for them to be given more and more functions. Intercommunion grows and gradually the dividing lines between denominations become less distinct.

This drift toward the nationalization of Protestantism is more than counteracted by the Ecumenical Movement. The trend toward a supranational Protestantism, indeed toward a supranational Christianity of world dimensions is so strong that it is overshadowing the dangerous proclivities toward nationalism which one phase of co-operation seems to encourage. The leaders of all these national organizations are so thoroughly committed to the Ecumenical Movement and that Movement is so gaining in strength that national particularism is being weakened and overcome rather than intensified.

The growing strength of the Ecumenical Movement in transcending national boundaries has been seen vividly in and since World War II. Early in the war the International Missionary Council instituted the Orphaned Missions Fund for the support of missions cut off by hostilities from their supporting constituencies. Through it British and American money went to Germans, and Presbyterian, Methodist, and Congregational money to Lutherans. American Lutherans gave generously to German Lutheran Missions. The fund was maintained after the cessation of hostilities. Emergency aid was provided in relation to every known situation in which it was physically possible to send assistance. Regardless of nationalities or denominations the

Protestant Christians of the world have stood together to insure the perpetuation of the spread of the Christian faith. Thanks to the Ecumenical Movement, the connections between Protestant Christians severed by war have been more quickly resumed since World War II than they were after World War I. Indeed, it is accurate to say that they were not spiritually broken but merely physically interrupted by World War II. The fashion in which within less than four months after the Japanese surrender Protestant Christians of the United States resumed communication on terms of entire cordiality and great joy witnesses to the strength of the tie knit through the Ecumenical Movement. Similarly the ease with which Germans, Norwegians, Dutch, British, Frenchmen, and Americans met with augmented fellowship in February, 1946, in the committees of the International Missionary Council and the World Council of Churches was in striking contrast with the difficulties encountered after World War I. The Ecumenical tie had grown.

Here, then, a new kind of Christianity is emerging out of historic Protestantism. Through Lutheranism, Anglicanism, and, to a less extent, through the Reformed churches it is maintaining connections with the long development of the Christian Church. Its swing is toward the radical wing of Protestantism and away from the accretions of the past. The swing is not so far as to mean divorce. Historical continuity is preserved. Then, too, the stress placed by the extreme Protestants upon the New Testament and the Christianity of the first century is a guarantee that the trend does not mean a departure from the Gospel but a firm resolution to emphasize it. Yet here is flexibility, the promise of encouraging the eternal Gospel to break out in new as well as in old ways, a pulsing life which is less constrained by the conventions inherited from the past than in any other form of Christianity. Here, too, through the Ecumenical Movement in all its various aspects is a form of Christianity which is achieving a more comprehensive Christian unity than the world has yet seen.

What the Christianity is to be which issues from Protestantism we cannot now know. Eventually it may be very different from anything with which we are familiar. As Protestantism came from Roman Catholicism, Roman Catholicism from the Catholic Church of the Roman Empire, and that church from primitive Christianity, perhaps there will spring from Protestantism still another major form of the faith. It may come by sharp revolution. It seems more likely to be through a development which will be marked by less of controversy and more of love than have most of the major changes in the past. It seems clear, however, that through Protestantism lies the main course of the Christianity of the future.

VI

Ultimately the future of Protestantism lies not in the trends and the movements we have mentioned. These are important. But, as in all Christianity from the beginning, continuing and growing vitality depends upon the degree to which Protestantism is a channel of the eternal Gospel. Protestantism came into being chiefly because through its great spirits the Gospel found fresh outlet. The revivals which have marked the course of Protestantism have sprung primarily from the same source. Other factors, some political, some economic, some personal, have been partly accountable. The most powerful and the one without which the others would have been impotent is the Gospel. In a continuing and growing loyalty to the Gospel in understanding and in full and joyous commitment is the hope of Protestantism. If Protestantism embodies the Gospel it will go on and grow. If it loses it or becomes too stereotyped to give it free expression it will dwindle and the eternal life in the Gospel will break out elsewhere and create for itself fresh channels.

That Protestantism will provide such a channel is the confident hope of many of us who have been nurtured in it and know it. Through it the power of the Gospel has come into our own lives. Moreover, the nature of Protestantism is such that more than any other form of Christianity it can take advantage of all that has been accumulated by the saints in the long history of the faith. More than those of any other branch of Christianity Protestants are drawing on the true treasury of the saints. The thought of the great minds of all communions is studied by their scholars. The works of meditation which are the deposits of the seers and mystics of all branches of the Church are the familiar possessions of those of them who are most deeply versed in the Christian life. Their hymnology knows no ecclesiastical barriers but takes toll from Eastern and Roman Catholic sources as well as from all the varieties of Protestantism.

Just now the numerical and material strength of Protestantism are mainly in the United States. World-wide Protestantism may well gain fresh insight and dynamic from what the Christians of Europe have learned of the Gospel through the sufferings of their tragic era. As, after the Thirty Years' War, minorities in Germany and from Moravia and Bohemia experienced afresh the power of the Gospel and contributed it to the Christians of the then most prosperous Protestant land, Great Britain, so in the decades ahead European Protestantism—yes, all of European Christianity—may fertilize the Protestantism of the United States and through it the Protestantism of the world.

Now as in the first century it is the Christian dream and the Christian opportunity that

All things are yours: whether Paul or Apollos, or Cephas, or the world, or life, or death, or things present, or things to come; all are yours; and ye are Christ's; and Christ is God's.

CHAPTER VIII

THE ULTIMATE SPRINGS

THE ultimate springs of the Christian faith are the Gospel. Here lies the continuing power of Christianity. If the Gospel were not timeless, if it did not meet the needs of men of all eras and cultures, Christianity would perish. It is because the Gospel is ageless and because it condemns men's sins, draws men to repentance, and opens the way to mastery over sin and to eternal, abounding life that Christianity has survived the death of culture after culture which it has helped to build and with which it has been associated, and, released from the thralldom of that connection, has, after a period of adjustment, gone on to fresh achievements.

Christianity is not the Gospel. It is a partial expression of the Gospel. It is a religion. Like other religions it is molded by its environment and to some degree reflects the age and the social, economic, intellectual, and political conditions in which it is set. It takes many forms. As do other religions it owes its distinctiveness in part to its cultural setting and in part to the dynamic which gave it birth. What separates Christianity from other religions is to some degree the cultural heritage with which it has interacted and of which it is the vehicle. It is now associated predominantly with the stream of culture which we know as Occidental. Yet its inner dynamic is not that culture, but the Gospel. The Gospel is the secret of its vitality. It is the Gospel which primarily distinguishes Christianity from other religions. Upon the Gospel depends in the last analysis the continuation of Christianity.

In any attempt to forecast the future of Christianity we must endeavor to put into words the essence of the Gospel. In the last analysis the survival of a particular form of Christianity depends upon the degree to which that form gives expression to the Gospel. If, then, we are to know the kinds of Christianity which are to continue or through which the main stream of the faith is to go on we must know what the Gospel is. Particularly if we ourselves are to contribute to the persistence of Christianity and to the giving of the Gospel to men we must seek to understand and commit ourselves fully to the Gospel. We ourselves must be manifest fruits of the Gospel.

It seems presumptuous to offer another statement of the Gospel. That has been essayed countless times. Creeds and confessions of faith have sought to put it into words. Books and articles beyond man's counting have been written on it. Moreover, the Gospel can never be fully expressed in words. It began in a Life and as a Life. It continues and, from its nature, must continue primarily in lives. It cannot be captured by any verbal formula or imprisoned on a page.

Even though to some degree the Gospel could be put into words it is too rich to be confined in any one utterance. Our Lord used many parables to illustrate it. Yet no one of them completely incorporates it. He himself was the Gospel, yet no one account of him adequately describes him. There are four books which we traditionally call Gospels. Each of them takes advantage of still earlier records. Each of the four and each of the sources which it uses presents our Lord from a different angle. The other books of the New Testament similarly offer great variety. For instance, the contrast between the letters of Paul and the Johannine epistles, and between them both and the letter of James are obvious even to the most casual reader.

Yet, impossible though it may be, we must here attempt again to put down in cold print what the Gospel is. We must add another to the untold thousands of written descriptions of the Gospel. Only from that vantage can we presume to look into the future to the near and far outlook for Christianity and for mankind. Only on such a basis can we hope to discover what, if anything, we can do to help shape that future. We must realize that what we here say cannot be complete or final. We must enter upon our task with deep humility. We must not try to rule out of the household of God those who cannot subscribe to what we put down nor resent those who are grieved by it as inadequate. Yet, we trust, there is in this statement something of the truth, a reflection, even though pale and distorted, of the reality which is too great for any one mind or heart. We must seek to know that love which surpasses knowledge.

I

At the outset we must remind ourselves of the meaning of the word "Gospel." It is simply the Anglo-Saxon, for Good News, or Joyful Message. It goes back, of course, to the Greek εὐαγγέλιον. It is "good tidings of great joy."

The New Testament rings the changes on that note. The stories of the birth are filled with it. It is the spirit of the *Magnificant,* of the *Benedictus,* of the *Nunc Dimittis,* of the announcement to the shepherds, and of the angelic song. The oldest of the Gospels has it in its very first line. Jesus compared himself and his disciples to a wedding party. There is the joy over the sinner who repents; the feasting and the joy over the return of the lost son; the joy of the one who, seemingly by chance, when he was not looking for it, discovers the treasure hidden in the field; the joy of the pearl merchant who has made it his business to seek and then finds; the joy of which we hear on the eve of the crucifixion and which was left as a legacy to the disciples. There is the joy of the resurrection, when the disciples were so full of it that they could scarcely believe what they had seen. After they could no longer meet their Lord in the flesh, the early disciples kept that same experience of joy. They "rejoiced with joy unspeakable." One of the outstanding "fruits of the spirit" which they found working in them was joy.

The word "joy," we must note, has a deeper connotation than the word "happy." It is akin to the term "blessed" which Jesus applied to those who had found or were finding true life. Joy knows pain and sorrow and yet is of such a nature that it is enriched through them.

So, through the centuries since, men and women of many races and stages of culture have found this same joy. Martin of Tours, who as a soldier gave himself wholly to Christ and left that occupation to be a pioneer in the monastic way to which he believed that dedication called him, impressed by his joy those who were attracted to him. Bernard of Clairvaux sings of "Jesus thou joy of loving hearts." Francis of Assisi and his early band were the troubadours of God, joyous in spite and in part because of their self-assumed poverty. Luther is a herald of joy. In his overcrowded ship to the Indies Francis Xavier is an incarnation of joy. John Wesley is found by the Gospel and becomes its messenger to an England that had partly forgotten it. In the nineteenth century John Bosco is a bearer of it among the underprivileged lads in Turin and through it gives rise to a new order. Wilfred Grenfell embodies it as he serves the fisherfolk of Labrador. Moody is captured by the "Good News" and in unlearned language tells it to the masses. In simple, unsophisticated "Gospel hymns" his associates and thousands since have sung of the wonder which they have glimpsed. This joy is our privilege today. Through all the ages to come it will continue to be part of the Gospel. It will be of the essence of all forms of Christianity which really incorporate the Gospel.

The word "Christianity" never occurs in the New Testament. Gospel is there and it is the Gospel which gives rise to Christianity and which is the source of its vitality. So long as any branch or expression of Christianity is a channel of the Gospel it lives. When it ceases to be a channel for the Gospel it becomes sterile and withers.

II

But what is this Gospel, this "good tidings of great joy"? Jesus associates it with the kingdom of God. He preached "the gospel of the kingdom of God." A great new age was about to dawn: "the kingdom of heaven" or "the kingdom of God" was at hand. It was the message of the kingdom which he preached and which he displayed in his life. Obviously the kingdom of God is where God's will is done. It is where God reigns. That is clearly the meaning of the prayer which Jesus taught his disciples: "Thy kingdom come: thy will be done on earth as it is in heaven." Men could enter that kingdom now. They entered it one by one.

In parables and in pithy, vivid sayings, Jesus described the kingdom of God. It was already present. Yet it was also coming. When a man glimpsed what it meant he would value it more than all his possessions. Part, then, of the great joy is that God's rule, God's kingdom is being realized, that men can enter it here and now. It is God's marvelous good gift to men. Yet God does not, perhaps cannot constrain men to enter it. They must come of their own volition. The impulse which leads them to come is of God, but He waits for them to respond.

That, too, is the experience today of those who have been

gripped by the Gospel. They have entered the kingdom of Heaven. They—we—are even now citizens of the household of God. We find the doing of God's will to be life's highest achievement—to be true life.

III

The Gospel also means life, eternal life, a life which begins here and now and goes on forever. The word "life" was often on the lips of Jesus. It is again and again in the New Testament. To enter and even to see the kingdom of God men must be born afresh. In our modern parlance we sometimes speak of "the Christian way of life" or of "Jesus' way of life." Such expressions do not enter fully into what Jesus taught and what the New Testament seeks to put into words. Nor are they in accord with the experience of those who across the centuries have been found by the Gospel. The Gospel does not speak of "a way of life" as though there were several, each of which might be good, or of "Jesus' way of life"—as though the alternatives to it were other ways of life. Again and again Jesus and the New Testament speak of life as contrasted with death. A man may "find his life" or he may "lose" it. There is "the gate," a narrow one, and "the way," a hard one, that lead to life. The alternative, by the wide gate and the easy way, is "destruction." The clear implication is that the large majority of men miss real life. They are born physically and many of them live decently according to the patterns and the moral and social conventions of their day. They may even be members of churches. Yet they have not entered into "life." This is the great tragedy, than which there is no greater. A man either has "life" or he does not have "life." The implication is that if men take the usual and the easy course the end is "death," not merely physical, but spiritual death. The "natural man" misses life. There are not several ways of life or several kinds of life, each of which deserves the title "life." This does not mean that God has not spoken outside the Christian revelation or that He has not elsewhere given glimpses of what life means. We are assured that the Word which was made flesh in Jesus "enlightens every man" and that "every one who loves is born of God and knows God." Yet in Jesus this life is made manifest and is made possible for men.

Physical birth is not enough. A dark taint accompanies that birth and it can end only in death, death of the spirit as well as of the body. This the New Testament recognizes as axiomatic. This, we may also add, is confirmed by the facts as we see them. How that taint entered we need not now seek to determine. The grim and awful fact is there. We are born with a haunting sense of possible perfection, a desire for "life" which is part of our nature. Yet we are also born with tendencies which, unless overcome, make the attainment of that goal impossible. Indeed, because of their contrast with that goal and their rebellion against it, they can and often do drag us lower than the beasts. Some power outside ourselves must save us.

But the Gospel, the amazing "good news," speaks of a second birth by which men may begin a new and different kind of life, an endless life. For men, otherwise hopelessly crippled by the weaknesses, the imperfections, and the base desires which have come to them from their long physical ancestry, real life is possible.

That eternal life is described again and again. No one set of words completely and minutely sets it forth. As far as any one word can encompass it, it is love. If a man loves God with all his powers and his neighbor as himself, he will live. Indeed, that is life. Eternal life is to know God. He who loves is born of God and knows God, for God is love. He who does not love does not know God.

Love defies full definition. It must be seen and experienced to become real. It is more than emotion, but it includes emotion. Paul in the most famous of his passages characterizes it. It suffers long and is kind; it does not envy; it is not jealous; it does not boast; it is not self-assertive or rude; it does not insist on having what belongs to it; it is not easily provoked; it is made sad by evil and rejoices in good; it hopes and through its power seeks to create in the one it loves what it hopes for; it believes that this is possible; it bears delays and disappointments in the appearance of what it longs for in the one to which it attaches itself; it never ceases and never, discouraged, gives up. This is the love of God for men. It is illustrated in the father in the inimitable parable of the two sons, for the usual title "the prodigal son" ignores the fact that when the younger one eventually responds the father's love still goes out, although as yet unsuccessfully, to the elder son. It is this love which men should have for one another.

The qualities of "life" are set forth in what we call the Sermon on the Mount. Those who have begun "life" are at least partly aware of how far they are from fully realizing it. Indeed, a prerequisite of entering the kingdom of heaven is "poverty of spirit," the humility and sense of sin of the publican in the parable of the Pharisee and the publican. Pride and smug self-satisfaction are symptoms of dangerous illness which, unless checked, can issue only in death. Pride is the great and fatal sin. Those who "hunger and thirst" for the qualities of "life," who are merciful, who give themselves purely, without taint of self-seeking, in complete commitment, to God, and who seek to achieve peace have the qualities of "life." Obviously they will be misunderstood and even hated and persecuted by some who have not entered into "life." That is partly because of innate perverseness in those who have not been "born again."

To live is more than to adhere to a code of ethics. It prizes and conforms to the highest ethics that man knows. True life goes beyond outward conduct to underlying motives, to the innermost thoughts and purposes, and insures that these are without bitterness, revenge, coarseness, contempt, or dishonesty. It is positive, not negative. It is a life of freedom. It is not bound by ritual taboos, whether of food or drink or the observance of days. Yet it is not license or self-indulgence. Some, mistaking it for such, have missed life or wrecked it through antinomianism, a belief that they were at liberty to do anything and to ignore what the race has through long and bitter experience learned— what God has written into man's nature—self-control, reverence, chastity, honesty, and self-giving love. Those who have entered into life keep the moral law. They go beyond its formal requirements. Yet they do not do so with the thought of acquiring merit. They know that life is not the balance of a moral ledger, the excess of good deeds over bad deeds. In humility they know their failure to attain the high requirements of God's law. When they are really living they act not from a sense of duty but from love. "The love of Christ constrains" them. They love one another because God has loved them. They are moved by a great gratitude. Love works no ill to its neighbor, but, rather, positively works good.

Eternal life is lived consciously and primarily in the sight of God, trusts God for such food and clothing as may be needed, and always subordinates them to doing the will of God. Its ideal is to be like God, to be perfect as God is perfect. As Paul puts it, its goal is "to be filled unto all the fullness of God."

Life involves growth. Eternal life is only commenced this side of the grave. Here, as Paul recognized in himself, those who have "life" have only begun to live. They have not yet fully attained nor are they made perfect. They are "being saved." The life process goes on through eternity. Since eternal life is to know the eternal God, in ever-growing understanding, reverence, adoration, and love, since the goal is to be like God, eternity itself is presumably too short for the final attainment of the goal. The end is not, as in some religions, absorption into the Absolute, the extinction of the individual. Always there will be "Thou" and "I." Never will the living, loving soul be absorbed into God. Always there will be love, with growing insight into the living, loving soul of God. That love is in response to the creative love of God. Always, too, there will be the family of life and love, the beloved community, the communion of saints, the continued love for one another of living souls who have been kindled into love and so into life by the love of the eternal God.

In this eternal life is part of the marvel of the "good news." To us, apparently bound by the brief span of our mortal flesh, inheritors of an ancestry that is red in tooth and claw, grasping, sordid, self-assertive, self-indulgent, quarrelsome, tempted to a bestiality that is lower than the beasts because it has in it more of corrupt imagination than the beasts, cruel, scornful, revengeful, threatening the entire human race with physical, moral, and spiritual decay, and even with physical destruction, this eternal life is revealed and made possible.

IV

The Gospel, the "joyful message," is that this life is revealed and made possible in Jesus and that it is the gift and the work of God Himself. By grace, the unmerited favor of God, we are saved. "The wages of sin is death, but the free gift of God is eternal life."

Since man's beginning God has been seeking to make Himself known to man and to open to him this eternal life. But He respects man's freedom. Life is impossible for automata. Those who are to live must have the liberty of choice between life and death. Even God must stand at the door and knock. If He batters down the door He has made impossible that fellowship, that "supping" together which is of the essence of eternal life. By long wooing He won to Himself a small, continuing minority in one of the politically least significant of peoples. Through that obscure minority, only dimly and gradually sensing what He was trying to say and to do, but yielding themselves to Him so far as their limitations would permit, God prepared the way.

Having prepared the way by speaking in "many and various" ways through this minority, the prophets and those who heeded them, God at last spoke through His Son. Again language fails to express fully what was done. Language can only present in imagery the amazing fact. Jesus of Nazareth, born of a woman, at the culmination of the long spiritual history of the minority, was the lord and pioneer of life who brought life and immortality to light. He was the eternal Word made flesh, for all to see. In him was life. That life was the light of men. In the spoken message and the deeds but above all in the man himself was seen that life. His contemporaries saw and their hands touched "the word of life." Jesus went through the world trying to show men by discourse, parable, quick aphorism, and act what that life meant. He endeavored to disclose to men that if they would only reach out in faith a marvelous life of unsuspected health and power was possible. He selected from those who responded an inner circle of friends whom by love he sought to introduce to that life. By obeying his words, by doing what he commanded, men can enter into life. Those who fully commit themselves to him, who believe him in wholehearted devotion are "born again."

This is not the full story. More than teaching by words and

even by example was necessary. Men did not automatically respond. Men were so perverse that they not only were blind to life when they saw it before them: they hated it and sought to destroy it. Not all so hated it. But those who dimly sensed it were too confused, too little understanding, fully to comprehend. Dismayed, when the crisis came, they crumpled. The very men who by the long preparation given their fathers should have been the first to welcome the Word, the life, and the light, were angered by it. The inner circle whom Jesus gathered about him and who ought best to have sensed who he was and what he was doing did not actively join in the crucifixion, but they did nothing to prevent it.

The crucifixion followed. That first Good Friday seemed to mark stark failure, not only for man but also for God. God's way had ended in the Cross, in the triumph of the very darkness which the incarnate light was seeking to dispel.

But the first Good Friday was not the end. After it came the first Easter. Life broke the bonds of death. Physical death could not hold the life revealed by God in Jesus. Indeed, the very tragedy of the Cross proved the way, the essential way to life. Christ crucified is the power of God and the wisdom of God.

Again man's language and precise definitions fail. Yet the experience of men, within a few short days after the Cross and the resurrection, proved that in the Cross and the resurrection power had broken through which in a fresh way introduced men to eternal life. Through it men were being born again. They were new creations.

The generations since have corroborated and confirmed that experience. Men of all climes and cultures and ages and races have discovered that as they have reached out in faith to the God whom they have seen in Christ a power not themselves has begun to work in them to bring them to a new birth and to produce in them eternal life. They must strive for that life, but their striving in itself avails nothing. That life is the gift of God's love in Christ.

V

Men, even those who have entered the new life and who rightly think of themselves as Christians, often stand confused and blank before what in formal language is called "the doctrine of the Trinity." Back of that doctrine, however, is great and glorious fact. It, too, is part of the Gospel, of the amazing "good news."

To appreciate what lies behind the doctrine of the Trinity we must remember how it came to be. The story usually told is one of controversies, party strife, church councils, jealousies between individual leaders, and jockeying with terms. It is not pleasant reading and leaves one sick at heart and skeptical. Fortunately, this is not all nor is it the significant part of the story. Long before the dissensions and the ecclesiastical councils experience had disclosed the realities with which the later thinkers wrestled.

We must recall that the first Christians were Jews. From infancy their teachers had drilled into them the unity and sovereignty of God. "Hear, O Israel, the Lord our God is one Lord and thou shalt love the Lord thy God with all thine heart and with all thy soul and with all thy strength." The first of the ten commandments is: "Thou shalt have no other Gods before me."

To these Jews, thus trained, there came experiences which enlarged and enriched their knowledge of God and hence their conception of God. They had known Jesus of Nazareth. Those who had been with him most intimately, had lived with him day in and day out, had heard him teach, had seen him in his deeds of physical, moral, and spiritual healing, had known his struggles, had been with him in his temptations, had, afar off, viewed his death, and had been witnesses of him after his resurrection, felt constrained by the facts to apply to him the highest terms that they knew. He was Christ. He was Lord. And by Lord the earliest Jewish Christians did not mean a lord akin to the lords of the mystery cults. They used the term Lord as they had employed it when they applied it to God. He was still Jesus the Christ, risen and "at the right hand of God," but in some way he was also God. God was to them one. God was to them Father, the name which they had seen applied to Him in their Scriptures and which they had heard Jesus customarily use for Him. Yet from what they had known of Jesus they must, they felt, enlarge their conception of God to include him. The language which sprang from their lips was varied: "God was in Christ"; "In the beginning was the Word and the Word was with God and the Word was God. . . . The Word become flesh and dwelt among us, full of grace and truth"; Jesus is "the Son of God"; "the only Son of God"; He is the express image of his (God's) person." God is one but in ways which break through language and escape man's conception of Him must be enlarged to take in Jesus. The High God is Creator and Father. He is also Redeemer and as Redeemer He became incarnate in Jesus. This was the faith of the early Christians. It was part of the "good tidings." As it was for them, so it is for us. It can be our experience today.

But the early Christians, through their experience, had their conception of God still further enlarged and enriched. They found a Power working in them and their fellows. It was through that Power that they were convicted of sin; it was through that Power that they were moved to repentance; it was through that Power that they found they were born anew, a new creation, and had entered into the new life. Through that Power they were lifted out of themselves and could be greater and more potent than they had been before. Fruits appeared in those in whom that Power worked which they recognized as characteristic. They were enabled to overcome "the works of the flesh" and to show forth more and more "love, joy, peace, longsuffering, gentleness, goodness, faith, meekness, self-control."

The disciples named this Power the Spirit. Sometimes they called it the Holy Spirit, sometimes the Spirit of Jesus or the Spirit of Christ, sometimes the Spirit of the Father, sometimes the Spirit of God. They associated him, for the Spirit is personal, with what they had read in the Old Testament of the Spirit of the Lord or the Spirit of Jehovah.

The early Christians therefore thought of God as Father, as Son, and as Holy Spirit. They did not wrestle with the intellectual problems presented by their experiences. They knew these experiences to be real. Later generations, facing the same experiences, but also seeking to understand and to state in orderly, logical fashion what they had felt and seen and heard, endeavored to work out formulas and longer statements that would put into words precisely what had long been known.

Then came, gradually, in more explicit statements, the doctrine of the Trinity. The Christians knew God to be one. They could not believe in three Gods. Yet they had these experiences, these facts. Here is not the place even to summarize their problems, their discussions, or even their conclusions. They are important, but our purposes would not be served by going into them.

What we must say, although briefly and categorically, is that here, in this enlarged and enriched knowledge of God, is part of the "good news." God is not only Creator and Father. He is also Saviour, who entered into our life by becoming "flesh." He is also ever active in human life, bringing those who receive Him into the new birth, introducing them to the beginnings of eternal life and transforming into the moral and spiritual likeness of Christ those who will allow Him to do so. Moment by moment men may recognize His presence and find Him the great Companion of their way.

VI

The Gospel, the "good news," is not merely individualistic. It has much to say of the new birth, of eternal life, of the goal of eternal life as being filled unto all the fullness of God, of being perfect as God is perfect. It also, as we have said, speaks of the kingdom of God. It has to do with a community. The disciples were taught to say, not "My Father," but "Our Father." They were not to pray for "my daily bread" but "our daily bread." The great Christian commandment is love, and Jesus tied together more vividly than ever had been done before the love for God and the love for one's neighbor.

Out of the Gospel arose, then, quite naturally, the Christian community, the Church. It was the new Israel of God, the company of those who had begun eternal life. No one organization and no congeries of visible organizations is identical with the Church of Christ. Much as Christianity is a religion, a mixture of the Gospel with extraneous and transient elements, so the visible churches, the ecclesiastical structures which men see, have in them many elements and features which are partly irrelevant and even contradictory of the Gospel and of that Church which is the blessed company of all faithful people. However, just as the Gospel could not go on in history apart from Christianity, so it could not continue except in connection with some church, some visible community.

We must not describe the differences between the various

churches, the weaknesses, the distinctive features, and the contribution of each to the world at large and to the Christian community in particular.

We must say, however, that here in time there is the Church. It is divided both outwardly and inwardly. Many of the divisions are palpably in contrast with the Gospel and contradict it. Some of the most bitter controversies and the deepest gulfs are, as we have reminded ourselves, not between ecclesiastical bodies but within them. Yet in spite of this seeming—and real—lack of unity, there exists an underlying unity. There is a common Christian faith. The vast majority of Christians would agree with the description of the Gospel given in this chapter. They might use different language. Here and there they would wish for more explicit statements and definitions. Many would feel that some difficulties have been avoided or slurred over. Others would add, as essential, points which have not been included. A few would feel that they could not assent to one or more of the statements which we have made. Yet on what have here been given as essential there would be almost universal agreement. In all churches a family likeness is to be found. It arises from a community of faith and common experience.

Moreover, the Church is not merely within time. Like eternal life, it goes on beyond history. By far the longer span is on the other side of the grave. The communion of saints is within time. Through the Ecumenical Movement it is in our day progressively real. But it goes on beyond time. The Church is a society of divine origin which is already living beyond death. Eternal life, as a life of love of God and of one's neighbor, only begins here. Here we have merely a taste of its richness, a foreshadowing of what it is to be. The Church as we know it is the faint and imperfect beginning of the community of love, of worship, and of praise which even now exists beyond our present ken and which has an enlarging eternity before it. As through the ages its members increase in the knowledge and love of God and of His Son and are deepened, enriched, and ennobled by that knowledge and love, they also grow in love of one another. The unimaginable richness of that fellowship is part of the amazing "good news."

VII

To all this there may seem to be an anticlimax. The Gospel is set against a background of darkness. The word is the light of men but the light shines in the darkness. Those who have entered the kingdom of God are light, but light entails darkness. They are salt, but salt is in contrast with that which needs salting. Since "few there be" who "find life," those who do so are a minority. The majority go on to destruction. The New Testament has much to say of evil. It seems at times pessimistic: "men love darkness rather than light"; "You being evil give good gifts to your children." We are commanded not to be anxious about the morrow because "sufficient unto the day is the evil thereof." So much evil must be met before nightfall that we must not borrow trouble from tomorrow. Jesus and the New Testament speak sternly of judgment, of those who are cast "into outer darkness where there is weeping and gnashing of teeth." They recognize poverty and suffering. They know of man's inhumanity to man. They are aware of man's perverseness. They do not seek to dodge sin or suffering or what the learned call "the problem of evil." Indeed, the usual symbol of the Christian faith is the Cross. The Gospels give a large proportion of their space to accounts of the trial and the crucifixion—more than they do to the resurrection. It seems strange, therefore, to speak in the same breath of the Gospel.

Yet here is not an anticlimax. If we are to see the sheer marvel of the "good news" we must conclude rather than begin our account of it with the world in which it is set. It is true that Jesus and the New Testament never discuss the problem of evil in the terms of the philosophic schools. Part of the Gospel is that in the Cross God met evil and overcame it. His wisdom and His power and His dealing with men are never so clearly seen as in the Cross. Jesus of Nazareth, his birth, his life, his death, and his resurrection, is the central fact of all human history. It is more than a conventional reckoning which increasingly dates all events from before Christ and in the year of our Lord—B.C. and A.D. The "good news" is that God is not defeated by evil. He permits it. We can surmise some of the reasons. Others the wisest cannot know. But the Gospel is that in Jesus of Nazareth God met evil and overcame it and that He continues to overcome it. To all who take Jesus as Lord and Master he is also Saviour. In deed, word, and life Jesus reveals what God meant human life to be. He discloses the ideal life. But the Gospel is more than that. Were Jesus simply the exemplar of the ideal human life, if he simply set it forth, men would faint from discouragement and despair. Chained by their sin they can never hope to attain that goal. The revelation only makes more hideous man's present state. But Jesus does more than disclose that life. He declares that men can, here and now, enter eternal life. He marvels that men have so little confidence in God, that they have so little faith. If only they will have faith, they will be saved. Jesus sees so clearly the infinite possibilities of human life that at times he is almost impatient with men's blindness, their unwillingness to see and to venture. The Gospel is that through the Cross, the resurrection, and the fresh access of the Spirit which followed, a new age dawned. It is an age in which men as never before are introduced to eternal life, an eternal, growing, abounding, radiant life of love with the others who share it and with the eternal God. It is an age in which they are given power to live that life, to attain by progressive stages the goal for which they were created. That power is not their achievement or by their merit, but through the unearned love of God.

In the last analysis the Gospel centers about God. It is the gift of God. The wonder of it grows the longer we meditate on it and live in it. The eternal God, the creator and sustainer of the vast universe, who was here in the immeasurable time before that universe began, who will be here after the stars are cold, who is great enough to know the sparrow that falls and the flowers that last but for the day, who is far beyond our full conceiving, this God in His dealings with men is love. By high and stern commands He confronts them with what they may become. By judgment He warns them. Yet in Christ He has made it possible for them to enter a new life of eternal and growing fellowship with Himself. Through the continued presence and operation of His Spirit He seeks to convict men of sin, to accomplish in them the new birth, and to work in them for an ever-growing likeness to Himself. Here, against the background of the world's tragedy, is the wonder of the Gospel. Here is the realm, if men would but see and submit themselves to it, where God reigns and where His perfect will of love is done.

CHAPTER IX

THE FAR OUTLOOK. WHAT CAN BE EXPECTED
OF CHRISTIANITY AND THE WORLD?

WHAT is to be the end of the story? Will the Gospel finally prevail? Will it so permeate and dominate Christianity that that religion will fully incorporate it? Will that transformed and perfected Christianity win all men and bring all human society not only to obedience but to its likeness?

I

Much can be said to warrant a glad, affirmative answer. Our Lord and the New Testament appear to hold out a confident hope for this culmination. The prayer that Jesus gave his disciples and which, more than any other petition, the Church has been uttering across the centuries has in it "Thy kingdom come. Thy will be done on earth as it is in heaven." We would scarcely expect our Lord to teach these words if he did not expect them, when uttered in sincerity and faith, to be answered. That prayer contemplates God's perfect will as being done on earth among men, in this sphere as well as in the heavenly sphere.

The most comprehensive form of what is commonly known as the Great Commission, with which Matthew's Gospel concludes, seems even more explicit. The risen Christ commands the eleven remaining disciples in the familiar words: "All authority hath been given unto me in heaven and on earth. Go ye therefore and make disciples of all nations, baptizing them in the name of the Father and of the Son and of the Holy Spirit, teaching them to observe all things whatsoever I have commanded you: and, lo, I am with you always, even to the end of the world."

This command has given rise to much perplexity. By many it is held to be a late addition. It uses the baptismal formula "in the name of the Father and of the Son and of the Holy Spirit" which appears to imply a much more mature doctrine of the Trinity than we find in most places in the New Testament. It is certainly without exact parallel elsewhere in the recorded teachings of Jesus. It comes at the close of a Gospel, where it might easily have been an afterthought of a subsequent generation who, quite honestly and innocently, put into the mouth of Jesus the aspirations of the Christian missionaries of their day. Matthew's Gospel is, moreover, the most narrowly Jewish of all the Gospels. It emphasizes the importance of keeping the Jewish law. It is the only one which reports the words of Jesus in commissioning the twelve: "Go not into the way of the Gentiles and into any city of the Samaritans enter ye not: but go rather to the lost sheep of the house of Israel," and "I am not sent but unto the lost sheep of the house of Israel." In contrast, the scope is breath-taking. All nations are to be made disciples. They are to be taught all that Jesus had commanded his intimate group. This obviously includes the injunctions of the Sermon on the Mount in the extensive form given in Matthew's Gospel. The standards there are so high and seemingly impossible of attainment by the multitude that some modern scholars have insisted that Jesus intended them simply as an "ad interim" ethic, to be observed by the little community of his followers in the brief interval which he is held to have envisaged between his teaching and his second coming. Yet here is the explicit injunction to teach all men to observe what the inner group had been commanded.

Can all men be taught to love their enemies? Can organized

labor and organized capital be induced to love each other? That would be admirable, but it seems beyond the realm of possibility. Can the Communists, who maintain that religion "is the opiate of the people" be induced to pray "Our Father" and not only to forgive but also to love those whom they regard as "reactionaries" and whom now they "liquidate" when they can? Can the Communists and Nationalists in China be persuaded to love each other? Can those who fear the Communists be taught to turn the other cheek when they believe the Communists to be the aggressors? Can the untold millions who are impelled by the economic motive and one of whose major drives is the struggle for the means of subsistence learn not to be anxious for the morrow or for food and clothing? Can the multitudes of coarse men be educated to take such an attitude toward sex that in their inmost thoughts there will be no improper attitude or desires toward women? Even for the few the command, "Be ye perfect as your Father which is in heaven is perfect," is impossible of complete fulfillment. Can all men be brought up to that level? If the command were obeyed human society would be ideal. Good will would take the place of war. Full and glad cooperation would supplant the economic struggle among individuals, classes, and nations. The dream of such a society is so alluring that we know that it should come true. Man's happiness can be achieved only as it is realized, but is it not utterly fantastic to hope that it will become actual? Then, too, the command was given only to the eleven disciples. Does it apply to all Christians?

These difficulties are undeniably there. I, for one, regard them as challenges rather than difficulties. Personally, I believe the Great Commission to be the words of our risen Lord to his disciples, and not the creation of a subsequent generation. They are given in various forms in the Gospels according to Matthew, Mark, and Luke, and in Acts. They obviously constituted the burden of the concern of the risen Christ. In his short earthly ministry he had, properly, concentrated his energies upon recruiting a company from among those best prepared to receive him. Now these, equipped with the Gospel, were to go out with it to the ends of the world.

Yet, if I were to hold to the other view, that the Great Commission came out of a late first-century or early second-century environment, out of what a subsequent generation of Christians had come to believe was the mission of the eleven, it would to me be fully as amazing and compelling. It is evidence that the early Christians believed that this was the command of their Lord and that in formulating it they were true to his spirit. It is implicit in the Lord's Prayer: "thy kingdom come, thy will be done on earth as it is in heaven." In some manner, either by his direct words or from the contagion of his spirit, issuing from Jesus there was the impulse which constrained the early disciples, almost against their will as strict Jews, to reach out and make disciples of all nations. Obviously the author of the First Gospel believed that in his life in the flesh Jesus wished to confine his mission and that of his disciples to the Jews. That, as we have suggested, was wise strategy. In the brief time that he clearly saw he was to have, if his mission was to be carried on our Lord must concentrate his efforts upon gathering a small minority whom he could train. These could best be recruited from those prepared by the background of the law and the prophets. At best they did not understand him in his lifetime. He was too breath-taking, too revolutionary for them. Only after his death and resurrection, as they looked back across what they recalled of his life, his deeds, his teachings, his death, his resurrection, and, above all, the man himself, and meditated on them, did they really begin to understand him. Even then they only partly entered into the significance of what they recalled. After nineteen centuries of experience the Christian Church does not yet fully comprehend its Lord. Clearly, then, in his earthly ministry Jesus must confine himself as strictly as possible to the Jews.

Yet somewhere along the way—and the records join in declaring that it was after the resurrection—the disciples began to see that the mission of their Lord was to all men. They perceived that the genius of his teachings, of his death, and of his resurrection must be universal. Stephen glimpsed it and was stoned for his radicalism. Saul was at first angered by it and then, yielding to it, became its greatest early emissary. To the first Christians there was no inconsistency in the Great Commission at the end of the First Gospel. They saw that it rightly, yes logically, belonged there. If the Sermon on the Mount, and it is given most extensively in the First Gospel, is valid for the few, it must be presented to all men. God who makes His sun to rise on the evil and the good and sends His rain upon the just and the unjust must wish that all men shall have the opportunity to learn of life, presented so cogently in the Sermon on the Mount, and, if they choose, to enter it. The standards set forth must be valid for all men, whether or not they accede to them. They portray life as it should be lived. They reveal what man was made to be. They describe the only true life, "life" as contrasted with "destruction." That was our Lord's clear statement when, at the conclusion of the Sermon on the Mount, he contrasts the two houses, the one built on the rock of his sayings and the other, ignoring his sayings, erected on the sand. As one reads the sayings and comes back to them again and again, he realizes that if the individual and collective life of men were governed fully by what Jesus sets forth all would be well. God intended men to be that way. It is because men are ignorant of these standards or, knowing them, fall short of them, ignore them, or flaunt them that misery and disaster come upon them. That they are ignorant of them, or, having heard them, disregard them is the great tragedy. Since this is true, to bring all men to discipleship and to teach them to observe these standards must rest as an obligation upon all Christians and not just upon the eleven.

Since the Great Commission arises naturally and commandingly out of the life and teachings of Jesus and in its fulfillment lies the only road to life for men as individuals and for human society, we would expect it to be possible of being carried out. The great God who is love certainly is not willing that any should perish but desires that all should come to a knowledge of the truth. As creator and ruler of the universe, moreover, his will must eventually triumph.

Then, too, the course of Christianity, as we have briefly outlined it, appears to warrant that hope. As a factor in the life of mankind Christianity has moved forward by great pulsations. Again and again it has been threatened by the collapse of a culture with which it has been closely associated or into which it has entered as a creative factor. For a time after each collapse it has receded. Yet, after a pause, it has gone on to wider effects upon the race as a whole. In some areas it has not recovered the ground lost, but in others it has advanced and the total gains have eventually far exceeded the losses. The widest extension of the Christian faith has been within the past hundred and fifty years. Even in the turbulent decades since 1914 it has, in spite of losses, moved forward.

As a factor in human history Christianity is young. As we suggested in the first chapter, we are still in the days of the early church. As one contrasts the less than two millenniums that Christianity has been present with the long course of life on this planet, or of human life, or even of human civilization, they are very brief. Christianity has barely had time to begin to take effect. The Gospel standards are so high that men, with their weaknesses and sins, respond to them very slowly. A minority first is won to them. Then great groups give them a superficial acceptance. Only gradually does even the minority understand and approximate to them. They are too high to be fully attained in this short life. Yet, in the contrast with the other religions, as we have seen, Christianity continues to gain. The other religions are born, rise, spread, become senile, and either die out or slowly lose ground. Christianity alone remains young.

It would appear that Christianity, with long centuries, probably millenniums, ahead of it, will progressively bring mankind into obedience. As in the past, this will not be by steady forward movements. Crises will be encountered. Losses will be experienced. Yet recessions will be followed by fresh advances. The general direction will be onward.

II

On the other hand, a number of uncomfortable facts rise and stubbornly oppose this hopeful prospect.

First of all, we of this generation are suspicious of easy—or even difficult—optimism. Two world wars and their attendant and more basic revolutions have sobered us. We look back with mingled wistfulness and sophisticated scorn upon the complacent optimism of the nineteenth century.

The doctrine of progress is dated. It belongs to that short and relatively halcyon age of the Occident which intervened between 1815 and 1914. Even that century knew such conflicts as the Crimean, American Civil, and Franco-Prussian wars. Yet, compared with the earlier Occident, and especially the eighteenth century, and with the post-1914 era it was peaceful. For the Occident, equipped newly with the machines of the Industrial Revolution, the nineteenth century was increasingly prosperous. Into this scene came the theory of evolution. The optimism of progress appeared logical. Life was believed to have begun in simple forms and to have developed into higher and more complex stages. At the apex came man himself who, springing from lower organisms, was now supreme. He had become so through his superior intelligence. What hypothesis seemed so reasonable as that which gave man and civilization an indefinitely growing and blissful future? So ran the argument.

In our day science and the machine are feared as the Frankenstein Monster which turns on its creator and destroys him. Civilization may be hurtled back into worse than barbarism by the forces which man has evoked. As geology has disclosed great groups of animal life which, once dominant, disappeared (the dinosaurs are a notable example), so man, if unable to fit himself to the environment of science which he has brought into being, may become extinct. The nineteenth century witnessed only the first blooming of science and of the Industrial Revolution. Our generation is seeing their fruits. The fruitage is mixed. Some makes possible physical comforts beyond the wildest dreams of earlier generations. Much is inane, such as the use of airplanes to write on our skies advertisements of inconsequential drinks. Much more is sour, and still more is baleful. By a generation such as ours, all talk of the triumph of Christianity is heard with impatient incredulity. This is especially the case in Western Europe and the British Isles, for here the full weight of the tragedies of our day has been felt. In the Americas traces of pre-1914 optimism linger. In some respects, in its attitudes and conditions, the New World is now the Old World and the Old World of Europe has become the New World, a feared foretaste of what is to come universally. That

New World is far from attractive and is quite counter to the doctrine of progress.

In the next place, the Christian is sobered by Jesus and by the New Testament. Neither of these knows a progressive or automatic triumph of Christianity. Indeed, as we have said, the word "Christianity" would be unintelligible to them. They know the word "Gospel," but they anticipate no full victory for the Gospel within history. Jesus frankly declares that the large majority of mankind go on to destruction. He speaks of the end of the age and in his description of it there is tragedy, with the separation of the good from the evil and with weeping and fire for the latter. The wheat and the tares, he declares, are to be together until the harvest. There is a harvest when they are suddenly and finally dissociated by divine decree, but until then they continue and each grows. It may be pushing the parable beyond its intended meaning to stress the word "grow," but that term seems to indicate an increasing maturity and fruitage of both grain and weeds. The nature of each becomes more obvious as the harvest approaches. How soon Jesus believed that the harvest would come is a matter of controversy among scholars. Some hold that he expected it very soon. Others, citing such parables as that of the five wise and the five foolish virgins, contend that he conceived it as being delayed far beyond the time which popular opinion then assigned to it. The wise were those who, in waiting for the bridegroom, made provision for a long and unanticipated delay. So, too, can be read the warning to those who, like the servant who when his lord did not come when expected, became negligent and abusive. Clearly Jesus foresaw the early destruction of Jerusalem and its temple, as any clear-headed man must have done as he viewed the seething, irrationally fanatical spirit of rebellion against Rome and knew the might of Rome. Whether he held that the full end of the existing human order would come within a short time is at least highly debatable. Obviously he could speak only in figurative language. For an event so far beyond human experience only imagery could be employed. Yet it is clear that he expected an end and that good and evil would go on together until, by His intervention, God judged and triumphed.

To many of the early disciples, perhaps to the overwhelming majority, the early return of their Lord was an inspiring hope. That return would mean the victory of Christ. Right would prevail and God's will would be fully done. Of that they had no doubt. A new heaven and a new earth would appear in which righteousness would dwell. But had any one suggested that this would come by slow stages and without the sudden irruption of divine judgment they would have looked at him in puzzled incomprehension. The gradual evolution of a perfect order would have been to them an entirely alien idea.

The breath-taking stature of the Christian ideal combines with what we know of human nature to deny the hope that Christians will teach all men all that our Lord commanded the inner group of his disciples. It is true that those commands commend themselves to our consciences at their best as setting forth what man should and ideally might become. Yet even by those who have been introduced to eternal life they are not fully attained in this life. There is in men in general, moreover, that dark side of rebellion, pride, and self-assertiveness which refuses assent to them, or at best renders them only lip service. Even if all men were to give assent it is utterly impossible that human society would fully incorporate them. After a brief span of sixty, seventy, or eighty years men leave this flesh behind them and go on to the next stage of existence. Even the saints have attained only the initial stages of the "high calling of God in Christ Jesus." If eternal life involves eternal growth we cannot expect human society fully to conform "within history." Lower ideals could be attained. Some religions have set up standards which are conceivably realizable this side of the grave. It is characteristic of the Gospel, and part of its glory, that it is set in both time and eternity.

The experience of history also forbids the complete fulfillment on this planet of a society which perfectly conforms to the standards of the Sermon on the Mount.

It is quite within the realm of possibility that in the course of many centuries all men can be induced to accept the Christian name and receive baptism. We have seen that occur in some countries. Christianity would then become the professed religion of the world.

Even this stage must be thousands of years in the future. The resistance of the elder faiths, Hinduism and Buddhism, is as yet almost unbroken. Few converts have been won from those castes in India which are most committed to Hinduism, or from those populations in Burma, Siam, Tibet, and Mongolia which are solidly Buddhist. The younger religion, Islam, gives still less indication of yielding. Secularism and the acids of modernity have done more to undermine these religions than have Christian missionaries. Communism is aggressive and is making headway. The defections from the churches in Western Europe are a retreat from the time when all except the Jews were baptized as a matter of course.

Yet, as we have seen, Christianity has been planted among almost all peoples. Much of this has been within the past century and a quarter. In view of the vitality and record of Christianity it is entirely conceivable that a few thousand years hence, if the human race and the planet last that long, Christianity will be the faith of the world community.

However, the record thus far shows that in nominally Christian countries full obedience to the commands of Christ is far from being realized. Indeed, some of the agelong evils of mankind have attained their most colossal dimensions within what was once known as Christendom, the area in which Christianity was the religion of the community.

This was true of Negro slavery. The devastation wrought in Africa by the raids and wars which fed the slave trade, the ghastly miseries of the trans-Atlantic passage of the victims, and the cruelties on the plantations of the New World for sheer magnitude are the outstanding example of the exploitation of one race of mankind by another. The slavery of the ancient Greek world and of the Roman Empire may have involved more millions. It certainly lasted longer. Yet it was not primarily a racial matter and it was not as extensive geographically. The depressed classes of India far outnumber the totals of Negro slaves at any one time and their condition has endured longer than did Negro slavery in the New World. Yet they, too, are more limited geographically and the members of those classes are not the chattels of the higher castes as were the Negro slaves of the whites.

Although Negro slavery has now been abolished in the New World and is all but extinct in Africa, as a legacy it has left race tensions which for gravity and geographic extent are as serious as any that the world has known.

Persecutions of the Jews have not been confined to Christians. Thousands were slaughtered in the Roman Empire and in Moslem lands severe disabilities were placed on members of the unhappy race. Yet more have been done to death in the past two centuries in Russia when it was officially Christian and, latterly, in a Europe which had long esteemed itself Christian than in any equal span of time in the world's history. We must recall, as well, the deportations centuries back from "Christian" Spain of both Jews and Moriscoes.

The only world wars which the race has known have either arisen in what was once Christendom and have been mainly waged there or have centered there. Some of the wars of the eighteenth century which were fought in Europe and its colonial dependencies extended to all five continents. The wars of the French Revolution and Napoleon were almost exclusively among professedly Christian peoples but touched not only every continent and many of the islands of the sea but also affected to a greater or less extent every major land. What we usually think of as World War I began in Europe and there wrought its chief destruction. World War II had its real inception in Manchuria in 1931 outside "Christendom" and between non-Occidental "non-Christian" nations, but it broke out in its fullest force in Europe and the chief weight of armaments involved was in nations which had long been under Christian influence.

To be sure, some earlier wars in which Christians were either not involved or only slightly involved were fully as destructive of life and property in particular areas. That, for example, was true of the Mongol invasions and the exploits of Tamerlane. Some of the wars in supposedly peace-loving China have led to a greater proportionate decline of population than did the Japanese invasion of the 1930's and 1940's. The extent of the world wars of "Christendom" has not been due to a greater ferocity of "Christian" peoples. It is assignable primarily to the expansion of Europe and to the machine, both of which have beneficent aspects.

Yet the fact remains that these world wars in which Christians have been prominent have been more extensive than any in which Christians have not been prominent. Christianity has not prevented them. Indeed, if Christianity is to any degree responsible for the machine and for the expansion of Europe it must bear part of the onus for the extent of these wars.

We must remember, too, that the churches themselves bear evidence of human imperfections. The record of their quarrels and of the self-seeking of their leaders makes unpleasant reading.

Moreover, we must note that, although it has spread more widely and has influenced more of mankind than has any other religion and is growing both in its extent and in its effect upon mankind as a whole, Christianity tends to die out in some lands where it has been longest present. It is almost as though it were a passing fashion. Its critics or enemies might compare it to a prolonged epidemic which eventually wears itself out. In the land of its birth it never had more than the nominal allegiance of the majority. It is now held only by dwindling minorities in Asia Minor, the first large area in which it became the faith of the majority. In spite of a remarkable vitality, it is losing ground numerically in much of Europe, the region in which it has had its longest course.

In other words, the pessimism of our generation, the attitude of Jesus and the New Testament, the nature of the Gospel, and the record of experience combine to belie the hope of the progressive winning of all mankind to full conformity to the life set forth in the Gospel.

Does the Gospel, then, tantalize man by an ideal which haunts him and will not let him rest but which he cannot hope to attain? Is this part of the misery of man, that God has implanted in him discontent with anything short of what Jesus set forth as inherent in his being, and yet that none but a few can hope to attain it, and they only beyond history, after they have passed through the gate of physical death? Will Christianity even pass the way of other religions and be left behind on the weary march of mankind, a noble vision but impossible of attainment? Is human history meaningless, full of sound and fury, signifying nothing? Or, what is almost as bad, is man hopelessly derelict, irredeemable even by the grace of God? Is the prayer, "Thy kingdom come, thy will be done on earth as it is in heaven," never to be answered? Is it a futile cry? Were Jesus and the early Christians deceived by their enthusiasm when they climaxed the Gospel story by the commission to teach all that Jesus had commanded them?

III

If history discourages the hopes of those who look forward to an automatic achievement on this planet of a society which will be perfect when judged by the standards of the Gospel, it also counters the despondent fears of the pessimists.

Nor is the conclusion to be the familiar and safe compromise, so beloved of cautious academic minds, between two extremes. It is, rather, that the course of humanity is to be viewed partly from time and partly from eternity.

We must once more remind ourselves of what we have so often pointed out, that in geographic extent, in rootage in the many tribes and nations, and in its effect upon mankind as a whole, the course of Christianity has been forward, and especially in the last century and a quarter. Far from dying out, Christianity, so history leads us confidently to predict, is in its youth and is to continue to mount as a factor in the human scene.

To reinforce this view, we must point out that if some of the hereditary evils of mankind attain their most colossal dimensions in the areas longest under Christian influence it is not because of the greater depravity of those who have borne the Christian name. Indeed, an assertion that these nominal Christians are more ferocious or more debased than the worst of pagans could not be substantiated. The wider dimensions of the evils are due to the larger part of the earth's surface controlled by Westerners.

Moreover, it is in the areas where Christianity has been longest in operation that the most daring and successful efforts to combat the traditional evils which beset mankind have been found. In almost every instance, when traced back to their roots these efforts are found to have had a Christian origin. The abolition of Negro slavery is a striking example. It stemmed primarily from the awakenings in Protestantism in the British Isles and the United States. Earlier the Christian conscience in the Roman Catholic Church placed on the statute books of Spain the Laws of the Indies to protect the aborigines of the Americas and the Philippines from heartless *conquistadores*. The Christian faith stimulated the first notable efforts to put the relations among nations on the basis of law rather than force and gave the vision and courage which lay back of the development of the peace machinery of the nineteenth and twentieth centuries. In an earlier chapter we have noted the achievements of the Christian faith in thought, in education, and in medicine, nursing, and public health.

Here is a kind of progress, even though not as automatic or as unqualified as that dreamed of by the now derided nineteenth-century liberal optimists.

This history contains no guarantee that the efforts inspired by the Gospel to counter man's collective ills will prevail. It is now fashionable, and rightly so, to speak of atomic energy. The application of this instrument in war may well end civilization as we know it and reduce the human race by more than half. Yet thus far, viewed across the millenniums, mankind has made progress and in recent centuries, as Christianity has gained in extent and momentum, an increasing proportion of the progress must be attributed to the Gospel. Should a major reverse overtake human civilization but in such form that not all mankind perishes, the trend of history thus far warrants us to believe that recovery will come, even though slowly, that in it Christianity will be a major factor, and that the faith will go on to fresh victories.

The New Testament, we recall, also contains ground for hope for mankind "within history." We read that "where sin abounded grace did much more abound," and that "the earnest expectation of the creature waiteth for the manifestation of the Sons of God" and "the creature itself shall also be delivered from the bondage of corruption into the glorious liberty of the children of God." We are assured that the darkness never puts out the light. We are encouraged by the prayer, "May the God of hope give you all joy and peace in believing, that you may abound in hope through the power of the Holy Spirit."

The standards set up by the Gospel are too high to be attained within man's brief individual life or within societies made up of men of short year-span. Yet this does not preclude progress toward them. Each individual must for himself enter eternal life but nurture in Christian homes by Christian parents gives children born and reared in them a start over those not so born and reared. As these homes multiply, each oncoming generation will have an advantage over its predecessor. History is not a meaningless succession of cycles as so many of the pre-Christian ancients held. As the Old Testament and New Testament seers perceived, it moves to a culmination. The contrast between the pagan views and the Christian insight was made vivid, once for all, in Augustine's *Civitas Dei*.

Should the world and the human race go on indefinitely, we can confidently expect Christianity to continue as a growing factor in its life. Mankind will never fully attain to the standards of the Sermon on the Mount. Both the high character of those standards and the conflicts in human nature forbid that hope. Yet we can expect larger approximations to be made toward them, by individuals, by groups, by the Church, and by society as a whole.

IV

What forms Christianity will take in the far future we cannot know. That, too, depends upon how long the earth endures. We have suggested that no one kind of Christianity can be regarded as normal or as final. The more stereotyped varieties, those most anchored to a cultural heritage of the past, will have the advantage of resistant tradition and structure, but the disadvantage of inflexibility and association with patterns which have been discarded elsewhere. Christianity will go in expanding influence through those forms which combine fidelity to the Gospel, the largest expression of the fruits of the Spirit, and adaptability to changing environments. We have seen reasons for believing that in the next stage of human history Protestantism will provide the main channel for the Christian stream. It will not be the only channel. Especially will the Roman Catholic Church continue and expand in geographic extent. Nor will Protestantism as we know it be the final form. Part of the promise of its growing future lies in the new movements which are modifying it and which may in time transform it. As the decades multiply and become centuries and as the centuries accumulate in millenniums the Church of Christ as a factor in human history will be ever more influential. It will draw on the rich heritage of its long past. But ten thousand years from now, should the earth then be here and the human race be upon it, the prevailing types of Christianity will differ from those which

we now know. Of that we can be sure. What will be their organization, what their worship, and what their emphases are hid
from our eyes. That they will still be witnesses to the Gospel
and that in them the characteristic fruits of the Spirit will be
seen we can be confident.

v

Sometime the world will end. Eventually the human race will
disappear. That may come by a sudden catastrophe, and perhaps
fairly soon. This seems to have been the expectation of the
Christians of the first century. It may be by the slow loss of air
and water. Adverse climatic conditions or an alteration in the
atmosphere may gradually work such untoward conditions that
mankind will no longer be able to maintain itself. This is the
trend of prophecy from modern science. Or mankind may destroy itself by its own sin and folly. But sooner or later human-
kind will no longer find a home on this planet.

What then? Will Christianity perish with the race? Here the
Gospel has an unequivocal answer. Its fruits will go on forever.
The religion called Christianity will vanish with the race. The
lives transformed by the Gospel of which it has been the vehicle
have eternity before them. What their condition will be we who
are now in the flesh cannot imagine. We are bound by time,
space, and matter. We must join with the ancient disciple in
confessing: "Eye hath not seen, nor ear heard, neither have entered into the heart of man the things which God hath prepared
for them that love him." Yet as we have again and again reminded ourselves, the "good news" has as one of its unchanging
essentials eternal life, begun here and now and continuing endlessly. It is not absorption in God as pantheism would hold. It is
fellowship with God and with others who have also entered into
eternal life. There the fruits of the spirit will be fully matured.

There the course which began in history will have its fruition.

We need not apologize for this faith as other-worldly. Rightly conceived it makes, not for relaxation of efforts to better conditions here and now, but it intensifies them. Any institution or practice which harms lives with an eternal destiny must be fought, because its consequences are infinite. Any effort which will enrich life, as the Gospel presents life, will call forth the highest endeavor. Human beings, even the lowliest, take on dignity because potentially they are heirs of God, joint heirs with Jesus Christ. If it is true to the Gospel, Christianity is both the most intensely this-worldly of religions, bending its energies resolutely and hopefully to improving conditions here and now, and the most other-worldly, with the highest of all convictions of the destiny of man.

The hope and the strength of Christianity are in God. God governs history. God must triumph. The time and the place of the accomplishment of His will are in part contingent on man's response. But God's will must and will be done. God is love. His love, which led Him to give His only Son for man's redemption, will not be frustrated or thwarted. It must prevail.

My thoughts are not your thoughts, neither are your ways my ways, saith the Lord. For as the heavens are higher than the earth, so are my ways higher than your ways, and my thoughts than your thoughts. For as the rain cometh down, and the snow from heaven, and returneth not thither, but watereth the earth, and maketh it bring forth and bud, that it may give seed to the sower, and bread to the eater: So shall my word be that goeth forth out of my mouth: it shall not return unto me void, but it shall accomplish that which I please, and it shall prosper in the thing whereto I sent it.

CHAPTER X

THE OPPORTUNITY OF OUR GENERATION

WHAT does all this mean for our generation? These pages will be read chiefly by Christians who are earnestly committed to their faith. Others will probably either not see them at all or will little heed them. The large majority of the readers will, too, be Protestants. What, then, do this history and this analysis have to say to Christians within the Protestant fellowship?

Obviously the situation is urgent. It is urgent for every generation. It is true of each generation that without it all its predecessors cannot "be made perfect." Every generation of Christians, moreover, has the opportunity and the obligation to acquaint their contemporaries with the Gospel. Yet our age is peculiarly critical. Clearly this is true if, as many Christians believe, our Lord's return is imminent. If they are right, the time is short in which to prepare their fellows for that event. It is also true if, as most Christians hold, the world is to go on into an indefinitely long future. We have seen the threats to the Christian faith which in our day have assumed such gigantic proportions. We also know the menaces to civilization itself before which the thoughtful of our day stand in palsied and futile fear. We are aware, too, that as never before it is possible to acquaint men the world around with the Gospel. The many means of communication—the radio and the airplane, added to the seemingly more prosaic contributions of earlier days, the printed page, the railway, the steamship, and the automobile—

make physically feasible the reaching of all men. Christian communities in almost every land and among almost every tribe and nation provide, as never before, nuclei for the spread of the faith. The disintegration of cultures carries with it in many lands the lessening of resistance to the Gospel. This is notably the case in Africa south of the Sahara, in Japan (perhaps only temporarily), and in China.

For our generation of Protestant Christians the opportunity and the attendant obligation are peculiarly imperative. The duty of Protestant Christians, as of all Christians, has always been to live the Christian life to the full. But the situation today emphasizes this duty. The position of Great Britain, still strong, and of the United States, now outstanding and both of them predominantly Protestant lands, gives to Protestant Christianity a reflected prestige which, though un-Christian and therefore perilous, can be utilized to make the Gospel known. If our analysis is correct, if, for the reasons we have earlier outlined, the main stream of Christianity is more and more to flow through the Protestant channel, then Protestant Christians are especially charged with the privilege and the duty of making their branch of Christianity really representative of the Gospel in all its fullness, for the sake both of those now living and those who are to come. We must not, if we are true Christians, take satisfaction in the lag of the Eastern churches and the somber future of the Roman Catholic Church. We must, rather, rejoice at every sign of the fruits of the Gospel in their ranks. But the responsibility for the continuing growth of Christianity seems to rest increasingly on Protestants. If we neglect our opportunity Christianity will not perish. It is far too vital to disappear because of the dereliction of any one or two generations of its adherents. It will go on. Yet if Protestants do not rise to the challenge of today Christianity may be partly crippled, with infinite loss to millions now living and to other millions as yet unborn.

What then should Christians, and particularly Protestant Christians, now do? What steps shall they take? What programs shall they adopt? What dreams shall they cherish? Above all, how shall they so lay themselves open to its power that the Gospel may have free course through them?

Christians, if they are true to the genius of the Gospel, must dream and act in superlatives. They must think in large dimensions geographically. Theirs must be the vista of eternity. They must be content with nothing less than the perfection of God, whether for themselves or for their fellows.

I

First of all, we must aim at nothing short of the complete fulfillment of the Great Commission. We must seek to make disciples of all nations, teaching them to observe all that our Lord commanded the inner group of his first followers.

We have seen how breath-taking is this vision. We have seen, too, the paradox involved, the paradox most vividly set forth in the Gospel in which the most comprehensive and explicit form of the Great Commission is given, between the hard fact that few find the way to life and the command to teach all men so that they may find it.

Late in the nineteenth century courageous youth in the Student Volunteer Movement for Foreign Missions adopted as their watchword "the evangelization of the world in this generation." By this was meant a giving of a knowledge of the Gospel to all then living. That watchword was criticized for being impracticable. Yet it is not as comprehensive as the Great Commission. It does not include making actual disciples of all peoples, baptism, or teaching all men to observe all that Jesus commanded. Our Lord and the early Christians were far more daring than the inspired youth of the optimistic late nineteenth century.

Although few find the way to eternal life, to be true to the spirit of their Lord Christians can aim at nothing less than making disciples of all men and teaching them to observe all that their Lord commanded them. Even if the Great Commission were not there in explicit words, it is implied in the Gospel. Those who have been introduced to eternal life, the life whose dominant feature is love, cannot rest content while any have not known or have missed the way to life. If the alternative to life, as Jesus plainly declares, is destruction, then the love which is of the essence of that life must endeavor to call all men to repentance and to the entrance into that life. William Carey, the shoemaker-teacher-preacher of the English Midlands, thought and planned in terms of the entire globe. The Welsh farmer's son, Timothy Richard, dreamed of conversions by the million in China and worked at projects for making this actual. Hudson Taylor, frail of body, felt the burden of all China laid on his heart.

Whenever any group of Christians has, for whatever reason, lost sight of the command to make disciples of all nations or has given up attempting to obey it, that group has become sterile. It has either died out or has continued to exist as a semimoribund community. That was long true of the Syrian Christians of South India. It has been the status of the ancient Eastern churches in the Moslem world. It was recently the condition of the Mennonites in Europe. To be sure, the attitude of each of these groups is understandable. Probably none of us under their circumstances would have done better. Each was surrounded by a society which at best tolerated the existence of dissenting Christian minorities and at times persecuted them. Any effort to win converts would be met by renewed and sharp persecution which would threaten the very existence of the group. Each, then, felt constrained to content itself with rearing its children in the faith. Yet gradually the children and the children's children became formal and compromised with the world about them. Similarly, those groups who have held to a form of the doctrine of election which forbids all efforts to win others to the faith have become static and have tended to die out. For its very life the Church must seek to bring all men to be disciples of its Lord.

The command is peculiarly relevant to Christians of our day. The trend, as we have earlier suggested, seems to be away from seeking to make disciples of all the nations and toward emphasis upon Christians as a minority in a hostile world. This, too, is understandable. True Christians have always been a minority. Those who have found the way to life have ever been few. For centuries, however, the majority of Europeans were baptized and thought of themselves as Christians. Their Christianity was superficial. Most of them had not found life. Always there were those who sought to fulfill all the requirements for eternal life. Thus arose monasteries and sects. Yet in a community which called itself Christian those fully committed to Christ were not always such palpable strangers as they are in many lands today. Some of them were accorded great honor as exemplars of the life which all professed to follow but which few seriously undertook. Today, because of the phenomenal spread of Christianity in the past few decades, in most non-Occidental lands Christians are small, even though growing minorities. The missions of our period have placed higher standards for admission to the Christian community than were customary after the first three or four centuries. They have sought to win individuals rather than the masses. In Europe, the traditional heart of Christendom, hostile forces have been aggressive and the percentage of professing Christians has shrunk. The faith of those who have remained true is probably more virile than that of the majorities of an earlier generation, but the trend is for Christians to be minorities. Only in the Americas and the British Dominions and, especially, in the United States, where more of the nineteenth-century world persists, does the contrary condition maintain. In the United States, as we have seen, the percentage of church membership is rising and mass conversion is still in progress. In general, Christians of today are more self-conscious minorities in an unfriendly world than at any time since the first three centuries of Christian history. We are, therefore, in danger of accepting that position and of being content with it. In some Protestant circles, often of the most earnestly Christian, there is much talk of creating "cells." The parallel is drawn from Communism. If, as in Communism, this means the multiplication of groups of those who, fully committed to their cause, seek to permeate all society with their ideals, the spirit of the Great Commission has been caught and is being implemented. If these "cells" are willing to become encysted, on the defensive against a hostile environment, then the spirit of the Great Commission has been lost and much of the essence of the Gospel sacrificed.

Shall we aim at the mass conversion of the world? Shall we welcome such community movements into the Church as were seen during the "conversion" of Europe and are being witnessed today among the black folk of Africa, in some of the islands of the Pacific, in the depressed classes of India, and in the United States? Obviously this leads to a superficial Christianity in which the level of Christian living is low. We in the United States have vivid evidence of it in the gross religious illiteracy of the majority of church members. Only a few have even an inkling of what is meant by eternal life as the Gospel

reveals it. Most confine it to a vague belief in God and a type
of morality which is approved by their fellows.

Or shall we seek primarily a full commitment to the Gospel
and admit to the churches only those who obviously have entered upon eternal life?

In general, the advantages of mass conversion seem to out-
weigh the disadvantages. The disadvantages are clear. We have
seen them in Occidental society. Someone has sardonically suggested that the inoculation of Europe with a mild form of Christianity effectively prevented it from catching the real thing. The
contrasts within the Occident between the standards of the
Gospel on the one hand and the life of individuals and of the
community on the other are obvious. Yet appeal could be
made to those ideals to which in theory all gave assent. Men's
consciences were troubled by the inconsistencies. Out of the
mass acceptance of Christianity came such efforts to approximate
to Christian standards as that of Hugo Grotius who in the preface to his famous *De Jure Belli et Pacis* declares that he was impelled to write the treatise by the spectacle of Christians killing
one another. Early in the nineteenth century Czar Alexander I,
moved by the Christian faith, appealed to his fellow monarchs
of Europe to base their relations with one another "on the sub-
lime truths which the Holy Religion of our Savior teaches" and,
because they also professed to subscribe to that faith and dared
not offend by refusing, they gave their nominal assent. From
that precedent, near the end of the century Czar Nicholas II
called the first of the Hague conferences. This constituted an
important step toward larger international co-operation. Could
all the world or even a very large proportion of it concur on
principles of conduct, and especially those outlined in the teachings of Jesus, the realization of world order, so desperately
needed, would be set forward. Even though the principles were

honored more in the breach than in the observance, the world would be better off for having given them formal assent. One reason for the international chaos of our time is the lack of agreement on criteria by which to judge right and wrong. Moreover, society would be more wholesome if the rank and file of individuals accepted Christian standards of conduct as authoritative, even if they did not nearly live up to them.

The mass conversion of mankind now seems a remote possibility. The recent losses in Europe, the Communist resistance, the secular spirit, and all the other obstacles and threats which we earlier outlined preclude the hope that all mankind will in the next century or even in the next few centuries give assent to Christianity. In some widely scattered lands and communities the majority seem to be moving into the Church. The United States, Negro Africa, the depressed classes of India, the Karens of Burma, and large portions of the Pacific Islands and of the East Indies appear to be among them. If the Christians of the many different areas of the globe can be conscious of being one in fellowship, in purpose, and in faith they can exert a large influence upon the affairs of mankind.

Moreover, if we are true to the Great Commission we cannot rest content with anything short of bringing all of human life into full conformity with the precepts of Jesus. We are enjoined to teach all nations to observe all that our Lord commanded his immediate disciples. This must include relations among nations, relations among races, the economic activities of mankind, the family, amusements, the realm of the intellect, the fine arts, and every phase of the multiform life of mankind.

Full achievement of the ideal is palpably out of the question. If the nominal acceptance of the Christian name by all the human race is only a distant dream, how far beyond the realm of actuality must this other be.

And yet, if we are true to our Lord, we must never permit the impossibility to become an excuse for resting content with less than perfection.

Moreover, if we "attempt great things for God and expect great things from God," much more will be accomplished than we had once dared to dream. Our Lord stressed the illimitable possibilities of one human life if only it gave itself in faith. Because he saw so clearly what man might be, he marveled at man's unbelief. Here and there in the history of the Christian faith there have been those who have demonstrated what seemingly ordinary lives can become if once they venture out in faith. Within ten years Francis Xavier set in motion forces which affected India, Japan, and China. Inspired and empowered by a full commitment to the Gospel, William Wilberforce addressed himself to the elimination of the international commerce in slaves. The prospect seemed hopeless, for the trade was firmly entrenched and was lucrative. Yet he succeeded. Samuel J. Mills, from the family of a country parson in New England, died in his middle thirties, yet, wishing to make his influence felt to the remotest parts of the earth, helped to set going movements which ultimately affected all the continents. Within his lifetime he had touched, directly or indirectly, India, the Mississippi Valley, Hawaii, and Africa.

The implementing of the Great Commission, then, means that, even in this adverse age, we must plan concretely and comprehensively for presenting the Gospel to all men and for endeavoring to make Christ's commands the rule for all phases of civilization.

II

We must also greatly strengthen the Ecumenical Movement. That Movement, as we have seen, arose in large part from the effort to carry out the Great Commission. It is because this can be best fulfilled by all Christians working together that men and women brought into being the various bodies which are the organizational expressions of that Movement.

We of our generation cannot determine the ultimate form which the Ecumenical Movement will take. Indeed, it is to be hoped that there will be no ultimate form. Such a form would mean that eventually the Ecumenical Movement would become stereotyped and ossified. That would be sterility and death. We can, however, contribute to the next stages of the Movement and help to determine its scope and its spirit.

As we face the Ecumenical Movement we must remind ourselves of several of its characteristics. It is still very young. It is already more inclusive ecclesiastically than any effort toward Christian unity which the Church has known. Because of its variety and its inclusiveness it is quite without precedent. Some of us are profoundly convinced that through it the Spirit is endeavoring to say something new to the churches. Or perhaps it is more nearly accurate to say that through it the Spirit is accomplishing that for which He has long been striving but has heretofore been hampered by human blindness or because the fullness of time had not yet come.

What can we do to help forward the Ecumenical Movement? Especially what can we do to aid it to accomplish what God wishes of it?

First of all we must be humble and teachable. We must not hold to our own vision of it as necessarily the final word of God for it. We must not identify it with any form of organization which is peculiarly dear to us or seek to confine it to a program which appears to us to be compelling. This is not easy. Each of us thinks in terms of patterns with which he has become accustomed. Those of us who have been reared in the extreme wing of Protestantism, and especially in denominations congregationally organized, are suspicious of the historic episcopate and of much that has come through what is often called the Catholic tradition. Those of the Reformed tradition find it hard to tolerate types of ecclesiastical bodies which do not have an orderly and visible set of church courts and a strong confession of faith. To them the Anglicans are more understandable than Baptists, Disciples of Christ, or Friends. To Anglicans the historic episcopate is essential. They may esteem it as of the essence of the visible Church or they may regard it as the form of church government upon which the centuries have placed their approval as best suited for the Church. But they cannot easily conceive of a church without a bishop. Some Protestants insist on organic church union, the merging of previously distinct ecclesiastical bodies. To others such organic union is anathema. They are willing to co-operate but are profoundly convinced that mergers will do harm to the Gospel and violate a sacred trust which has been committed to their particular denomination. All of us must seek to learn from one another and from God. We must have ears to hear what the Spirit is saying to the churches.

That does not mean that we are to be without convictions. We must form them with all the honesty, the unselfishness, the intelligence, the daring, and the vision that we can command. But we must not be so wedded to them that we believe them to be God's final word or regard ourselves as infallible interpreters of God's will. As in the past, so in the future, the Ecumenical Movement will presumably have a variety of organizational forms and from time to time will develop new ones. We will see mergers of existing denominations and more and more fellowship among Christians of differing confessions and increasing co-operation among denominations. We will also witness the formation of new denominations, some of which will not co-operate with the others. No one of us is wise or far-seeing enough to perceive what the precise picture or even the main outlines of the Ecumenical Movement will be two generations or even one generation hence. We must certainly not attempt to dictate what it shall then be.

We must always remember that salvation does not come primarily through organization. Our Lord gave almost no attention to organization. The structural forms of the Ecumenical Movement, as of the Church in general, are only means for the carrying out of the Great Commission and must always be kept ancillary to it.

In the second place, we must not be content until the Ecumenical Movement is true to its name. It must be as inclusive as the inhabited world. As we suggested a few paragraphs above, it must seek to implement the Great Commission. It must have as its objective making disciples of all the nations and bringing them into full conformity with all that our Lord taught. That is clearly an impossible assignment. Yet to be true to our Lord we must not dream or plan in less daring and comprehensive terms.

This means what we have customarily termed evangelism, seeking to introduce men and women to the eternal life revealed through the Gospel.

Much of this will be through personal friendship, through the costly self-giving love which can be poured out only on the few.

Clearly, too, we must strengthen what we are accustomed to call foreign missions. The small minorities of our fellow disciples in non-Occidental lands, the "younger churches," must be assisted in their mission of evangelism by representatives of the "older churches." In some countries, notably in China, Japan,

Korea, the Philippines, Burma, and the East Indies, the "younger churches" have undergone terrific suffering and the loss of a large part of their physical plants. They need continuing aid from the "older churches," but given in such fashion as to strengthen them and their ability to stand on their own feet rather than to make them permanently dependent on the churches of the Occident. The rootage of Christianity among non-Occidental peoples in leadership and initiative which we noticed as a feature of our day must be deepened.

Obviously what we generally term home missions must also be augmented. We have been told that the reconversion of much of Britain is imperative. Millions on the Continent of Europe are so secularized as to be in fact pagan. In the United States many areas exist, some in the cities, some in the rural districts, either completely untouched by the Gospel or so superficially reached that they are almost non-Christian.

The Great Commission means, we must repeat, attempting to bring all phases of the human scene into subjection to Christ. For some this will entail a concrete undertaking in one small community. For others tasks of geographically larger dimensions will be the answer.

The world-wide scope of the Great Commission must be within the purview of all the organizations which we regard as visible expressions of the Ecumenical Movement. They may specialize. For instance, the World Council of Churches at present tends to concentrate its efforts on the Occident and especially on Western Europe; the International Missionary Council takes the non-Occidental part of the world as its main field: yet neither must minimize the importance of the other's assignment and the fullest and heartiest co-operation must be maintained.

We must not be content until all Christians are in some

fashion brought within the Ecumenical Movement. This does not mean inducing them to enter one organization. Indeed, it does not need to wait for such an organization. For instance, it is so improbable as to be almost impossible that the Roman Catholic Church will ever join a World Council of Churches, or, on the other hand, that all non-Roman Catholics will conform to that church. Yet even now, in spite of tensions between ecclesiastical organizations, beginnings are seen of fellowship between Roman Catholics and Protestants which are of the essence of Christian unity. Some of this is in individual friendships. The more these can be multiplied the better. There are few of us who cannot have at least one of them. Some is through cooperation, as here and there in Germany, or in undertaking together common tasks, such as famine relief. None of these need be at the sacrifice of deeply held convictions. Reciprocal respect and deep affection are possible between those who profoundly differ.

Each of us Christians may to a large degree realize the Ecumenical Movement in his or her own life. This we may accomplish partly through living as Christians in the perspective of the entire world. All that we do in however small the neighborhood in which we reside can be consciously against a global background. In information, in thought, and in prayer we can be as inclusive as the inhabited world and be centers of that perspective. Our sympathies can be as broad as the entire Church. While entering into the life of a particular congregation and denomination, and the most effective "Ecumenical Christians" are so rooted, we can be understanding of the views of others and richer for them. The devotional literature of all is available to each of us. As we become familiar with it and allow it to feed our lives, we expand until we are in the communion of saints of all ages and branches of the Church. Not all of the devotional classics will appeal to us. Not every saint of the past speaks to our condition. Some will never meet our needs. Others will serve one mood but not another. Yet through growing and widening acquaintance we find our spirits enlarged. To a less extent we can enter into the public worship of the various denominations. Normally most of us will be bound by obvious duties to our own fellowship. On the occasions when it is possible to be present at the public worship of other denominations we will often find that lack of familiarity and of the overtones which long association brings leaves us uncomprehending and cold. However, for most of us occasional presence at another type of worship can be arranged. We can at least read the liturgies of other churches. They may not appeal to us, either in print or when witnessed. Yet we can be respectful, try to understand, and enter (sympathetic imagination will do much to aid us) into the feelings of our fellow Christians who find much of value in what repels us. Those of us to whom the sacraments mean little must seek to appreciate, so far as we may, the convictions and experiences of those to whom they mean much. Those who have been nourished on the sacraments must endeavor to comprehend how those who refuse to use even the word "sacrament" and for it substitute "ordinance" have come to that position, and how, without the sacraments, they find nourishment for their spirits. Those to whom the cults of the Virgin and the saints are repellent can discover in them, even when they cannot enter into them, a more vivid awareness of the vast and living company of those who have preceded us through the gate of physical death into the next stages of eternal life. The "communion of saints" can take on fresh and enriched meaning. In these and other ways each of us can be conscious members of the Ecumenical Church and find fellowship with some of its members who have not been and perhaps never will be brought into any organizational expression of the Ecumenical Movement. We may be only dimly or partially aware of the enrichment which will come to our own lives and still less conscious of the influence upon others and the contribution to the Ecumenical spirit, but by such individuals, multiplied by the thousands as the years pass, true Christian unity will be furthered more than by visible institutions.

For many of us the greatest obstacles to Christian unity are not our relations with members of other communions but tensions and dissensions within our particular denomination. That may be because we do not work so closely and live so intimately with those of other religious bodies. At present most of the bitter controversies which rend the seamless robe of Christ are not between denominations but within them. Particularly is this true of the clergy and of those laymen and women who are active in ecclesiastical bodies. The rifts between "fundamentalists" and "modernists," between the "neo-orthodox" and the "liberals," between Anglo-Catholics and their non-Anglo-Catholic brethren, between those who wish to enter into co-operative enterprises or church unions and those who do not are more acute than those between Protestant denominations and, at times, than those between Roman Catholics and Protestants. Yet if the unity of love of which the Ecumenical Movement rightly makes much is to be achieved, these rifts must be overcome. Christian unity, we need to remember, is not to be attained through organization. Organization can help: it can also hinder. Christian unity will inevitably take on organizational expressions, but it will never be identical with them. It is an achievement to which each of us can contribute, and often most effectively within our particular branch of Christ's Church.

Ultimately the contribution of the Ecumenical Movement, as of every other in the Church, will depend upon the degree to which that movement embodies the spirit and the power of Christ. Machinery and techniques must all be subordinated to this central purpose and mission.

III

Christians and especially Protestant Christians must discover afresh, and as never before, the riches in the Bible. In principle most Protestants regard the Scriptures and especially the New Testament as the word of God and as the authoritative guide to faith and practice.

Latterly the Bible has suffered. That has been partly through neglect. The religious illiteracy which is marked in our day, notably in much of the Protestant constituency in the United States, includes a colossal ignorance of the Bible. The simple text is unfamiliar to the majority. The dying out of family worship, the ignoring of the Bible in most of the schools maintained by the state and even in the curriculums of some of the colleges and universities which were originally on church foundations, and types of religious education which, "pupil-centered," have rejected the older forms which made much of the text of the Scriptures have combined to produce a lamentable unfamiliarity with even the passages best loved by earlier generations of Christians. Moreover, for many modern scholarship has thrown doubts upon the Bible. Some lightly dismiss the miracles or the story of creation and with them discount the entire book. Others, more seriously troubled, find difficulty in a book much of whose contents seem to them to be contradicted by science. In the past century or more the methods of modern historical scholarship have been directed to the Bible more intensively than to any other body of literature. The results have shaken older attitudes and theories of inspiration and for thousands among clergy and laity have detracted from the Book. Troubled, these Christians have wished to hold to it, but have not been able to readjust their use of the Bible in such fashion as to overcome the losses. Much of the Bible, therefore, is discounted or ignored. Many conservatives, pained and appalled by its fruits in the lives of some whom they have known, and angered by the conclusions, have vigorously rejected modern scholarship. In reaction, they have held to an arid verbal literalism which has narrowed the life of themselves and their churches. All this is so much a matter of common knowledge among those familiar with the current Protestant scene that we need not elaborate it.

What we must say is that we can and must take advantage of historical scholarship to release the riches that are in the Bible. All truth must be God's truth. Far from fearing honest, conscientious, and able historical scholarship, we should welcome it, confident that, rightly used, it will enhance the Bible as God's word. It can do this by making clearer the way in which God's Spirit used the human instruments to speak through them and by separating the human voices from the Divine Voice.

All this, too, has been said many times, but not yet have either the leaders or the rank and file achieved the goal. Far too many of the Biblical scholars, while competent in the words and dating of the texts and in ferreting out sources, are too absorbed in these details or too little interested in the eternal message of the Book even to help in the thrilling adventure. Students who sit in their classrooms either are won to an emphasis upon the technical processes or have their comprehension of the Bible further beclouded. This need not be. Much of our vaunted Biblical scholarship is poor scholarship.

A really great scholar, or even a merely competent one, if he is to deserve either adjective, must enter into the spirit of the originals. He must see as their writers and those whom they recorded saw, feel as they felt, hear as they heard. He must do more: he must discern back of what the writers saw, felt, and heard, the eternal Word. To do that requires insight, but it requires more. It requires personal knowledge of the eternal God, an abundant living of the eternal life revealed and made possible by the Gospel. Only a great Christian can be a great Biblical scholar, for only he can see both Old and New Testaments together and can really discern the fashion in which the former is fulfilled in the latter. Only he can really hear and comprehend what God is saying through His Word.

Such scholars are not made overnight. Nor is their appearance assured by our modern Biblical training. Indeed, much of that training cripples them by leading them into bypaths or into distorted emphases. Fortunately a few are beginning to appear. Fully familiar with the accumulated results of the technical scholarship of the past two or three generations and competent in methods, accepting the general principles although not all the conclusions of those methods, steering a straight course through the many dissident and therefore confusing findings, they have so clear an understanding of our Lord and are so fully committed to him and have been so caught by his spirit, that they make scholarship illuminate the Gospel.

Thanks to the work of Biblical scholars we are in a position better to comprehend Jesus and the Gospel than any generation of Christians has ever been. If we will but pay the price of dedicating ourselves fully to him and, in the light of that dedication, utilize what scholarship has made accessible to us, we can be channels for such streams of power from the Word of God that all of Protestant Christianity shall enter upon a new accession of vitality.

Let no man mistakenly suppose that this will be easy. It will not. Old attitudes are deeply entrenched. Old misunderstandings or partial understandings have the sanction of devout spirits of many generations and the support of strong ecclesiastical precedent and prejudice. Much, perhaps most, of modern Biblical scholarship is arid, far more than the older orthodoxy. Yet the Bible is the inspired Word of God beyond our present fondest imaginings. It will make itself heard. It is for us to tune our ears to hear. Having heard, we must act. We must do what God in His Word commands us to do.

We must make tributary to the Gospel not only Biblical scholarship but also all of the vast range of new knowledge brought to mankind by science. Some of this knowledge has been feared. It has been viewed with distrust because it is believed to undermine Christian faith. Or we have stood in terror before it because it can be employed for the physical destruction of man. Yet, so far as it is true it is God's truth. It can be utilized to enlarge our understanding of the sheer marvel of the Gospel. It can also be made to serve the cause of the Gospel in assisting in the realization of the abundant life. And by "abundant" is meant what is inherent in the confident assertion: "I am come that they might have life and might have it more abundantly."

This, too, will not be accomplished by any one or any facile program. Many must work at it. Yet it can be done.

IV

What Protestant Christianity needs; what all Christianity needs; what the world needs; what all creation waits for with eager longing is "the manifestation of the sons of God." It is through this that in the past each new forward surge of Christianity has come. It is through this that Christianity will go on to added power.

Always this "manifestation of the sons of God" has begun with individuals and small groups. A man or a woman has been captured by the Gospel and, radiant and compelling, has attracted others who in turn have become candles of the Lord. The procession is long. Stephen's face, reflecting the glory of God, haunts Saul, until he, stricken by the great light on the Damascus road, becomes a kindling fire. Through Paul flows the main stream of life which carried the faith to much of the first-century Mediterranean world.

On the eve of the decay of Rome Ambrose yields to the importunities of the populace, distributes his goods among the poor, and becomes Bishop of Milan. He permanently enriches the hymnology of the Church and by his preaching gives the final impulse which brings the brilliant but morally enslaved Augustine into the triumphant liberty of the children of God. All the Christianity of Western Europe, both Roman Catholic and Protestant, witnesses to the power of Augustine's mind and the depth of his new life through the Gospel. In the twilight of civilization in Italy, Benedict of Nursia gives himself fully to Christ, by his example attracts a band of followers, and sets for them an order of Christian living which becomes the model for other groups which in turn are beacon lights in the dark centuries of Western Europe. Francis of Assisi is captured by Christ and, in complete and joyous dedication, wins others who by word and example carry the Gospel to the populace in the growing towns and cities of Medieval Europe. Their successors in the Order of Brothers Minor have been or still are missionaries in every continent of the globe. Wyclif and his preachers, who set England ablaze, in turn inspire Hus, through him contribute to the Moravian Brethren, who through a spiritual succession, after seeming disaster, from their center at Herrnhut, a small community, become an inspiration to much of Protestant Christendom; Ignatius Loyola and the Society of Jesus committed "to the greater glory of God"; Fox and the Society of

Friends; John Wesley and his societies and his preachers; George Williams and his fellow clerks in the first Young Men's Christian Association; Robert Wilder and the Student Volunteer Movement for Foreign Missions—all these are but a few of the examples of individuals who, fresh manifestations of the sons of God and kindling centers of small groups, have contributed mightily to new advances of the Christian faith.

This is the opportunity of today. The Gospel is still here with all its amazing "good news." The kingdom of God can be entered. The world waits for those who will even now live as in the kingdom.

No hard and fast details can be laid down as to what that demands. The general outlines and the main principles are clear. They are found in our Lord's teachings. In an earlier chapter we have tried briefly to summarize them. Each must discover, in his or her particular situation, what is entailed. That is one of the challenges of the perfect law of liberty, the glorious liberty of the children of God. Clearly it means glad self-giving in love. part of the "good news" is that we are to live not under the compulsion of hard duty but under the compulsion of love. "We love him because He first loved us." Few there be, even among those who bear the Christian name and are sincere servants of our Lord, who rise above the level of "oughtness." Yet we are told that we are not to be servants but friends of Christ. That is the high privilege of those who have entered fully into eternal life.

Hope, faith, and love have long been recognized as the distinguishing marks of those who have entered the new life of the Gospel. In an older day certain virtues were listed which Christians should have in common with noble non-Christians. Faith, hope, and love were recognized as peculiarly Christian additions. Here was a valid insight. "These three" are distinguishing marks of those who have entered the new life in Christ. Never were they more urgently needed than in our day, with its sense of futility, its fatalistic despairing expectation of recurring and greater disaster through war, its time-limited perspective, its distrust, its hatreds, its *sauve qui peut* attitude. Yet the eternal Gospel is here for all who will respond.

Those who respond to the Gospel will forget themselves. They will lose their lives for Christ's sake and the Gospel's. They will learn to abide in Christ and so to bear much fruit. They will exhibit that combination of the life of prayer and meditation on the one hand and of enhanced, active, self-giving lives lifted quite out of themselves on the other which mark those who have entered into life.

Few if any of us have more than begun to realize what prayer can mean. It is as natural a part of true living as is breathing to the physical life. It is conscious association with the eternal God. It is characterized by a growing, glad seeking of the will of God, an increasing knowledge of God, not only a knowledge about Him but the knowledge which springs from intimate, adoring fellowship with Him. It can never be put fully into words. It is so keeping the commands of Christ that the Father and the Son make their abode in our humble dwelling. If that figurative language seems unreal it is because we have not entered upon the experience which it seeks to describe.

Those who have learned something of prayer find that the promise is true and that they actually do greater works than our Lord did in the days of his flesh.

The command to be perfect as God is perfect is not intended to depress us by the impossibility of obedience. It is a promise as well as a command. Paul's prayer for the Ephesian Christians that they might be filled unto all the fullness of God has in it confidence, confidence that it can be answered. The goal is beyond attainment in this present life. But there have been and still are those who are making such evident progress toward it that the discerning see in them the foretaste of what they are to be in the succeeding stages of eternal life.

It is to this that the Gospel invites us. Those who respond to the invitation are those through whom Christianity will persist. Their presence will determine whether the Roman Catholic Church, Protestantism, or some other form of Christianity not yet on the horizon will be the main channel for the Gospel. That Christianity will go on is certain. God will not be defeated. The precise form or forms which Christianity takes are relatively unimportant. The hour and the manner of God's triumph are partly dependent upon our co-operation. We are fellow laborers with God. But even the time and the way of God's victory are not of primary concern. It is of supreme importance that the Gospel in all its beauty and radiant power shall be revealed in human lives, in lives forgiven, cleansed, and transformed by the love of God which is in Christ Jesus our Lord.

Who will answer? Who will so open his heart to the suffering and the perils of our day that they will bring him to allow God to work through him. The word of God is not lacking. "The word is nigh thee." He who responds will meet persecution—as have those before him, as did Christ. He will know pain and disappointment. He will not transform the world. But he will become one of those who are the salt of the earth and the light of the world. He will be among those who hold the world together. He will be one of the eternal company who live even now in the kingdom of God against which the gates of hell shall not prevail in this world or the next.